Vietnam Travel Guide 2019

Ha noi City - The Third Journey

16 Tips For Amazing Trip

JASON NGUYEN

ISBN: 9781697701296

TEXT COPYRIGHT © [JASON NGUYEN]

TABLE OF CONTENT

INTRODUCTION

Referring to Vietnam, people often think about war. But now, Vietnam is a beautiful, peacef Referring to Vietnam, people often think about war. But now, Vietnam is a beautiful, peaceful, safe and hospitable country.

Did you discover Ho Chi Minh City? Enjoyed the wonderful beauty of Danang - Hue - Hoi An? It would be flawed not to visit Hanoi

Known as the capital of Vietnam, Hanoi is also one of the important cultural, political, commercial and tourist centers of Vietnam. Over a thousand years of history, Hanoi has become a famous tourist destination around the world.

In this book, you'll learn about:

✓ Things need to know before going to travel Hanoi

✓ How to move in Hanoi city

✓ Certain attractions must visit.

✓ The best time to visit a certain area.

✓ Great culinary discovery.

✓ Accommodation.

✓ Travel tips.

✓ And more!

This book is a comprehensive guide and i hope it will help you have a fun and hassle-free trip in Hanoi ul, safe and hospitable country.

Plan Your Trip

Well come to Ha Noi

Hanoi is the capital of the Socialist Republic of Vietnam, also the capital of most former feudal dynasties in Vietnam. Therefore, Hanoi history is associated with the ups and downs of Vietnamese history through the periods.

Different from the dynamic and magnificent Saigon, Hanoi pops up in the mind of each person as a peaceful with mossy old houses.

The city has the most monuments and landmarks

A land of thousands of years of history, Hanoi has deposited the cultural quintessence of the nation throughout the history of building and defending the country with more than 4,000 famous relics along with a treasure of intangible cultural heritage extremely rich.

The famous famous relics of Hanoi are Co Loa Citadel, Van Mieu - Quoc Tu Giam, One Pillar Pagoda, Hoan Kiem Lake, Ho Chi Minh Mausoleum, Tay Phuong Pagoda, Thang Long Imperial Citadel, Duong Lam Ancient Village ... Besides, Hanoi has also have many unique festivals and a diverse and unique culinary culture.

The only city in the world with 3 independent declarations

Ancient Thang Long and Hanoi today are the places to be honored to witness the formation of two immortal cultural works of two famous authors - two world cultural celebrities: "Binh Ngo Dai Cao" by Nguyen Trai in the early 15th century and President Ho Chi Minh's "Declaration of Independence" in the middle of the twentieth century. The two works above, together with the poem "Nam quoc Son Ha" by Ly Thuong Kiet, in the second half of the 11th century, were considered by historians to be the "Three Declarations of Independence" of the Vietnamese .

Also here on 2 September 1945, when President Ho Chi Minh read the Declaration of Independence giving birth to the Democratic Republic of Vietnam, two declarations of France and the United States were also raised at the same time. This is not only the harmony of the people of Hanoi, the people of Vietnam but also a special place that no place in the world has the honor and luck to have.

The best street food

On the rankings of the Telegraph (UK), Hanoi topped the list of 16 cities with the most delicious and rich cuisine in the world with a variety of delicious and attractive dishes such as bun cha, pho, bread pa -tê with cucumber herbs, broken rice with grilled pork ..

Whether coming to Hanoi at any time of the day, visitors can easily find suitable street food.

Ha Noi's Top 9 reason to love

Favorable Weather

Even though Vietnam is a tropical country with the signature dry and rainy season, but Hanoi is the most ideal city in Vietnam to characterize the tropical monsoon climate with four seasons: spring, summer, autumn and winter. For travel lovers, the various weather conditions in four seasons make them more eager to visit Hanoi many times in a year because it is like in four different places. Actually, each season has its own beauty and characteristics. However, the best time to visit Hanoi is in the autumn. At that time, the clear sky and the fresh atmosphere will make you pleased and relaxed.

Everything is Cheap

Capital cities are usually pricier than places inland. Hanoi is an exception to this rule as it's the only major city with a robust hostel system that also offer some great deals to surrounding landmarks such as Sapa Valley and Ha Long Bay. You also get fresh beer for dirt cheap at one of the many bia hoi joints in the Old Quarter. Most museums in the city are on the cheaper side as well helping you save additional costs while free attractions include the serene Hoan Kiem Lake, One Pillar Pagoda and West Lake where you can sip Vietnamese coffee and people-watch to your heart's content.

A diverse cuisine

Not only does Hanoi has a lot of beautiful landscapes but it is also famous for its uniquely diverse cuisine. The Telegraph of UK has ranked Hanoi in the first place on the list of the cities having the most impressive culinary cultures in the world.

"Vietnam once touched your heart will make you unable to pull out. When you have loved this country, you will love forever " by famously chef Anthony Bourdain when took Barack Obama in Ha Noi.

Owning the Old Quarter

This is the highlight of Hanoi. Visiting Hanoi Old Quarter, you will have a chance to wander all day on 36 streets for 36 trades. Also, you can contemplate the hoary beauty of old houses which still retain their appearances from the 19th century. Going to this place, you can explore the inherent peace of Hanoi as well as the beauty of Hanoi people through their simplicity and friendliness in their behaviours and dressing.

A mix of Eastern and Western architecture

Being the capital of Vietnam, Hanoi has a long history with the age-old traditional and cultural values. Also, it owns a large number of architectural structures reflecting the intercultural intersections between Vietnam and France. Some outstanding relics are National Museum of Vietnamese History, Hanoi Opera House, Presidential Palace and Long Bien Bridge. Some monuments and tourist destinations representing for Vietnamese history are Temple of Literature, Ho Chi Minh Mausoleum, Ho Guom Lake, Ngoc Son Temple, West Lake, Huong Pagoda and so on.

Visit Ho Chi Minh mausoleum

Hanoi is the only city in Southeast Asia with an embalmed leader on display. The real body of Ho Chi Minh lies preserved in his mausoleum, much against his own wish to be cremated.

Vietnam's beloved leader has been laying in state immaculately preserved since 1969.

Special Museum

The Vietnam War -- most iconic war? The Vietnam War is remembered as much for the atrocities that occurred as it is for the anti-war demonstrations abroad. It is a war that influenced a decade of youth culture in the U.S. and continues to inform pop culture around the world.

A trip around Hanoi will surely enhance you knowledge in the cultural and historical understanding of Vietnam. The city boast a wide variety of museums ranging from history to art so you can spend your time learning about the country's immortal stories.

Leap-of-faith traffic

Step confidently out on Hanoi roads. Crossing the road in Hanoi is unlike anywhere else.

The road traffic is crazy in Hanoi, but it is organized chaos and somehow pedestrians always make it to the other side.

On foot. It's a little bit like bungee jumping. You just have to believe it when people tell you "It's going to be alright, just keep walking!"It's a test of faith in fellow humankind as you step into moped madness, trusting scooters to avoid you as you cross the road - An extremely memorable experience.

Discovery

Hanoi is a great place to access some of Northern Vietnam most beautiful sites. From the city you can easily access the amazing natural wonders all around. Many tours to Halong Bay start from here, and it's easy to take the night train up to the highlands of Sapa. You can also take day trips to Tam Coc and the Mai Chau areas which will give you a glimpse of Vietnamese rural life. It's very easy to arrange tours in the city, and most hostels will offer you a selection of good value packages.

Need to Know

Currency

Viet Nam Dong (VND). All cash transactions with other currencies are illegal, except for licensed exchange places like banks.

Most places in Ha Noi deal only with cash. Some foreign credit cards are accepted in high- and establishments

Language

Vietnamese.

Time Zone

GMT plus seven hours (GMT +7).

Mobile Phones

Pre-paid SIM card is the simplest option for travellers - they are widely available and you can buy anywhere stores. They usually include both talk and data packages.

When to go

High Season (Mar-Apr and Sep-Nov)

A cool and dry season follows the monsoons.

Mar-Apr : The temperatures are warm and comfortable - The best time to travel.

Sep-Nov: This is autumn with Northeast monsoon, the weather began to chill - Suitable for sightseeing activities.

Low Season (May-Aug and Nov-Feb)

May to Aug is generally very hot and dry, the average temperature of Ha Noi is more than 30°C - sunburn and skin damage easily.

Nov to Feb is the Winter with drizzle - The weather is very cold and uncomfortable - Not recommended travel in this time.

Important Phone

Vietnam's country code (+84)

Emergency : 112, 113, 114, 115.

Hotline for Tourist : 1800556896

Daily Cost

Public transport: 5.000VND - 15.000VND

Boutique Hotel : 250.000VND

Meal/Street meal : 25.000VND - 50.000VND

Small bottle of beer: 20.000VND

Motorcycles hire: from 50.000VND/day.

Getting Arround

Bus popular and cheap for travel between towns

Car & motorcycle convenient and easy to hire for local touring.

Train slow but great for sightseeing.

Air fast but expensive.

First Time to Ha Noi - Things To Prepare

Identification – The most important thing you need to prepare before traveling.

You need to prepare passports and visa, airline tickets, hotel reservation, services. For children, it is necessary to bring birth certificates.

In addition, to be proactive in all situations, you should bring with you or remember some contact information (email, phone number, address) of relatives, hotel, tour guides or even embassies. It is also necessary to remember some hotlines.

Make sure your passport is valid for at least six month.

Select a tour or travel by yourself

This depends on what you expect from your trip as well as your money. If this is the first time you travel far away and don't have much experience, tours is a safe option for you, but if you already have experienced traveling abroad, wanting to explore freely but you don't have much money, travel on your own will be the best option. In case money is not a problem to you, special tours with many preferential services should be better choice.

Notify the bank of the time you will go abroad

This is one of the most important things you must do before traveling abroad. If you do not notify your bank about an overseas trip, the bank may assume that the transaction of your account in another country is unusual and suspicious. That may result to lock your card. What more horrible than can't use bank cards during vacation?

To ensure financial security when traveling abroad, you should remember:

● First, notify the bank the time and place you will travel

● Secondly, always carry a small amount of cash in case your card does not work.

Prepare multi-function adapter

Discovering new places is always a great experience but if your phone or camera is out of battery and you can't charge them, so you can not take pictures or make videos, it can be a disaster, making your trip terrible. Because the socket in each country isn't the same. In addition, your phone may be broken because of the difference between voltage sources. So, In order to protect your beloved electronics and not wasting time to go looking for a convertible outlet, you need to bring a multi-function adapter up for every journey.

Setting the communication network

If you travel alone but don't want to spend all your time alone, let's start making contacts with your friends before you leave, you may have unexpected companions. Just let many people know your journey as possible by creating a travel blog (such as Tumblr, this is a very good application because you can use hashtags to find people who have the same destination as you) and connect your friends on Facebook, Instagram, Twitter... In fact, most people like to meet and share their experiences with others.

Booking hotels and air tickets.

You should make a room reservation as soon as possible, especially on holidays, if not you may have to stay in the hotel not as expected or even have to pay double.

Do not believe entirely on photos advertised online or on hotel websites. You should carefully read feedbacks, reviews, comments of previous visitors about hotels that help you make the best decision.

Please refer to many booking sites, to find the best price. Some reputable sites such as: Booking.com, Agoda.com, TripAdvisor.com or some locations introduced by Vietnam Travel Guide 2019 below.

Booking air tickets, too. Airfare prices often change, depending on the time and price of fuel. Therefore, taking advantage of early flight bookings to enjoy incentives is a smart choice.

Sim card

If you stay in one country for a long time, you should buy a SIM card from that country. This SIM card helps you to contact friends (local), call taxi and using Wifi, without worrying about losing roaming charges. Be sure to carry a phone that is not locked, because you cannot install a domestic SIM card on the locked phone.

Good footwear, mosquito repellent and rain jacket

HaNoi's streets are bumpy and lumpy, so a good footwear is a good idea. If you come HaNoi in rainy season, rain jackets are indispensable, beside that mosquito repellent are also very necessary when coming a tropical country like Vietnam.

On The Road

Chapter 1: Arrive Ha Noi

From the Airport to Ha Noi

General information

Noi Bai International Airport is about 30km from Hanoi Center and has 2 passenger terminals:

→ Passenger terminal T1: serving domestic flights; including Vietnam Airlines, Vietjet Air and Jetstar Airlines.

→ Passenger terminal T2: serving international flights; including many airlines such as Vietnam Airlines, Korean Air, China Airlines, Thai Airway, Japan Airlines, Cathay Pacific ...

Special services available at Noi Bai airport:

→ Catering, duty free sales, gift shops

→ Baggage storage service, baggage packing

→ Bedroom service at Noi Bai airport

Noi Bai International Airport is connected to the center of Hanoi by two large bridges, namely Nhat Tan Bridge and Thang Long Bridge. These will be two main routes for passengers to travel from Noi Bai Airport to Hanoi.

Option 1: Take a Bus

1/ Buses of the airlines

All 3 domestic airlines: Vietnam Airlines, VietjetAir, Jetstar have buses to and from the city to Noi Bai airport and vice versa.

How much: 40.000VND/person (rather cheap).

Frequency: 30-45 minutes / trip

How long: Typically 45 minute to 1 hour, depending on traffic.

Time of operation: 05 am - 10 pm

For convenience, Vietnam Airlines also allows passengers traveling on domestic flights departing from Hanoi to check-in for free (check-in) at the bus stop. Therefore, when arriving at the airport, passengers will not have to redo boarding procedures and can enter the lounge immediately.

Option 2 : Take the public bus

There are 7 public bus lines run from Noi Bai Airport to Ha Noi Capital.

How much: 9.000VND/person.

How long: Typically 45 minute to 1 hour, depending on traffic.

Frequency: 15-20 minutes / trip

Time of operation: 05 am - 8.30 pm

Public bus prices are very cheap but will be very crowded, if you want to be comfortable and do not put cost issues first, you should use other options.

Option 3 : Metered Taxi

There are 12 taxi businesses licensed to operate at Noi Bai International Airport. Taxis are arranged to wait for guests at the first floor - public areas of stations T1 and T2.

How much: The taximeter operates by distance with a metered fare. On this journey, you'll also pay an airport tax 10.000VND. In total, the ride will cost about 280.000VND - 350.000VND depending on the location of your accommodation (rather expensive but very convenient)

How long: Typically 45 minute to 1 hour, depending on traffic.

Frequency: 15-20 minutes / trip

Time of operation: 05 am - 8.30 pm

Chapter 2: Accommodation in Ha Noi

Luxury Backpackers Ha Noi

Hanoi noisy and overwhelming? Not in this place. Very good located in the old French quarters but in a small street were car-traffic is not possible. This hotel is within a 10-minute walk of Hanoi Cathedral, Hoan Kiem Lake and Hoa Lo Prison Monuments. Thang Long Water Puppet Theater and Ngoc Son Temple are also within 15 minutes. It is a 16-minute walk from Hanoi Railway Station and 18 minutes from Long Bien Station, Hanoi.

Style: Private Rooms

Start at : $15.5 USD / 375.000 VND

Address: 56 Ngo Huyen, Hang Trong, Hoan Kiem District

Hanoi Tomodachi House

This hostel is located in a nice, interesting area. You will get picked up at the airport and that is a good idea. Good and variegated breakfast. Nice rooms and great service. Charming street and close to a lot of activities.

Style: Dorms/ Private Rooms

Start at : $15.5 USD / 375.000 VND

Address: 5A Tong Duy Tan , Hang Bong, Hoan Kiem District

Vietnam Backpacker Hostels - Downtown

Right in the heart of hanoi's old quarter, downtown hostel is the biggest hostel in Vietnam, and is known for its legendary bar. with nightly events, Downtown is a constant hive of activity . it's close to delicious street food, cheap Bia Hoi spots (local fresh beer) and pumping nightlife. The hostel has a bustling travel desk servicing full country travel planning ; along with a fifth floor hangout space, flush with a large tv, football table, pool table and computers.

Style: Dorms

Start at : $12 USD / 288.000 VND

Address: 9 Ma May, Hang Buom, Hoan Kiem District

Little Charm Hanoi Hostel

Extremely friendly and English speaking staff, clean facilities, and even a free unlimited beer happy hour. They arrange a multitude of tours around vietnam (Sapa, Ha Long Bay) and airport pickup/departure. You will have free walking tour Hanoi with the tour guides of hostel - been a great experience!

Style: Dorms/ Private Rooms

Start at : $13 USD / 312.000 VND

Address: 44 Hang Bo, Hoan Kiem District

Note: This hostel is often full of rooms, please booking rooms before you arrive to make sure get your room.

Hanoi Brother Inn & Travel

If you want somewhere to stay that is friendly, great location and amazing staff this is the place for you! Hanoi brother Inn is an exceptional hotel/hostel for the price. The staff are very kind and helpful and speak very good English! The rooms are big and you get exactly what you pay for, it's not the fanciest place you will ever go to but the location and staff make this a place you will return to!

Style: Dorms/ Private Rooms

Start at : $15.4 USD / 370.000 VND

Address: 21 Bat Dan, Hang Bo, Hoan Kiem District

Backy Posh Hostel

Looking for dorms? Stay next to Backy Posh Hostel. the hostel has a charming interior design, offers the most lux dorm beds, each with their own privacy curtains, electrical outlets, nightlight and super cozy comforter. The best thing about Backy is the fantastic team running it - They create a real family feeling here with loads of laughs but always maintaining super friendly service to every guest. You will love it.

Style: Dorms

Start at : $11.25 USD / 270.000 VND

Address: 3 Hang Tre, Hoan Kiem District

Ha Noi La Siesta Diamond

Very luxury. Staff all respectful pleasant and wanting to provide 5 Star service. Ha Noi La Siesta Diamond also gives you a bars at the rooftop with the best view down to Ha Noi old town. The family room was very clean. We feel very safe staying there.

Style: Private

Start at : $95 USD / 2.280.000 VND

Address: 32 Lo Su, Ly Thai To, Hoan Kiem District

Hanoi La Siesta Hotel Trendy

Very luxury. Staff all respectful pleasant and wanting to provide 5 Star service. Ha Noi La Siesta Diamond also gives you a bars at the rooftop with the best view down to Ha Noi old town. The family room was very clean. We feel very safe staying there.

Style: Private

Start at : $150 USD / 3.600.000 VND

Address: 12 Nguyen Quang Bich, Cua Dong, Hoan Kiem District

Chapter 3: How to Get around

Buses

This is the cheapest form of transportation in Vietnam in general and Hanoi in particular and it is also a fun way to see the city! Your hotel can help you sort out which bus goes where.

The advantage of using public buses is economy and convenience. Besides, there are countless limitations that need to be considered. Because buses are public transports, people use them a lot, during rush hour they can be full; Moreover, buses focus on many social components so there can be negative situations such as pickpocket, scuffle, harassment ...

Getting on the bus is not allowed to carry bulky goods and luggage. Many bus routes do not reach the destination directly, so you have to walk quite a distance to reach your destination. So don't use them if you're in a hurry!

Taxi

Always use the meter in a taxi! Once the meter is on, you can trust that he'll take you where you need to go. However, Sometimes you may still be driven around by the driver for extra fee.

Grab taxi

As I just mentioned, sometimes you'll have a little trouble with traditional taxis. Skip the headache and order a Grab Taxi who will run the meter honestly and will drive much safer than the traditional taxis. Especially, you can book a car anytime you want and the price is usually cheaper than traditional taxis (except rush hour).

In Vietnam there are many online taxi booking services for you to choose with competitive prices such as: Grab, Be, Fastgo

Motocycle

In Vietnam, motorcycles are the most popular vehicle. Riding a motorbike in Hanoi has many advantages such as helping you take the initiative, saving time and motorbike is also quite compact so you can move inside the narrow old streets of Hanoi.

If you rent a motorbike when traveling in Hanoi, you should note that you must ensure the car is still safe, still use well to avoid damage while traveling on the road. A travel experience in Hanoi by renting a motorbike is that you should negotiate the price before deciding to rent. When renting a motorbike, you need to bring a driver's license, a passport.

One thing to note when riding a motorbike in Hanoi is the parking space. You are only allowed to park in areas where motorcycles are allowed. If you do not pay attention, you may be punished by the Police. Before parking your car somewhere, you should ask about the price first and make sure they will keep it safe.

Bicycle

In a noisy, busy city where traffic congestion is common, bicycles are an excellent choice. This is a vehicle many tourists love to come to Hanoi, especially for foreign tourists. While cycling, you can just watch the streets and enjoy the attractive street food. If you are visiting Hanoi for the first time, try renting a bicycle to enjoy the most interesting moments in the capital.

Cycling is not only convenient but also contributes to protecting the environment, training and improving health. However, according to the experience of traveling in Hanoi by bike, you should also pay attention to preserving it well or it will be stolen. On bad weather days, cycling is not a reasonable choice.

Cyclo

Viewing and enjoying the landscape by cyclo is an interesting thing that anyone wants to experience when traveling to Hanoi capital, especially the old town. This way of traveling makes you feel new and come closer to the breath of life and culture of Hanoi.

Chapter 4: Attractions in Ha Noi

Ho Chi Minh Mausoleum Complex

Opening hours of Ho Chi Minh Mausoleum Complex

❖ In Summer (1 Apr - 31 Oct)

+ From 7:30 - 10:30 AM, 1:30 - 4:30 PM (Mon - Fri).

+ From 7:30 - 11:00 AM (Sat - Sun).

❖ In Winter (01 Nov - 31 Mar)

+ From 8:00 - 11:00 AM, 1:30 - 4:30 PM (Mon - Fri).

+ From 8:00 - 11:30 AM (Sat - Sun).

1. **Ho Chi Minh Mausoleum,** the place where Uncle Ho's remains are located. It was officially started on September 2, 1973 at the old stage in the middle of the historic Ba Dinh square - where Uncle Ho read the declaration of independence giving birth to the Democratic Republic of Vietnam on September 2, 1945. Ho Chi Minh Mausoleum is a place for people from all provinces in the country and those who admire him to come to burn incense to pay homage.

❖ **Entrance Fee:** Free

❖ **Address :** 02 Hung Vuong Street, Dien Ban, Ba Dinh, Hanoi.

❖ **Notes and regulations :**

+ Clothes:

This is a political and solemn place, so visitors should note: when you go to Ho Chi Minh Mausoleum not wearing offensive, pants or short skirts. To dress politely and neatly is a way of showing respect for the great Uncle Ho.

+ Attitude

When you enter the mausoleum, you need to go lightly, say quietly, line the way to visit. Avoid talking loudly, pushing, jostling because this will affect the order as well as the solemn atmosphere in here. Before entering the mausoleum, remove the hat from your head, do not put your hands in your pockets or pants, and show your standard attitude.

+ Items are carried and used

Guests are not allowed to film or take pictures when going inside. Mobile phones can be carried but need to turn off the noise and not make noise. In particular, to ensure the temperature, general hygiene of the tomb, you can not bring food or drinks.

❖ **Note :** According to the regulations of Ho Chi Minh Mausoleum, children under 3 years old are not allowed to visit.

2. Ba Dinh square

The square has a campus with a length of 320m and a width of 100m, with 240 grass plots, interspersed with a 1.4m wide walkway. In the middle of the square is a 25m high flagpole. This is the place where parades take place on the occasion of Vietnam's major holidays, and also a place to visit, have fun and go for a walk of tourists and residents of Hanoi.

Ba Dinh Square is the largest square in Vietnam, located on Hung Vuong street and in front of Ho Chi Minh Mausoleum. This square is also a place to record many important imprints in Vietnamese history, especially, on September 2, 1945, the President of the Provisional Government of the Democratic Republic of Vietnam Ho Chi Minh read Declaration of independence gave birth to the Democratic Republic of Vietnam.

❖ **Entrance Fee:** Free

❖ **Address :** Hung Vuong Street, Dien Ban, Ba Dinh, Hanoi.

3. House on stilts and fish ponds (Nhà sàn)

A very simple lifestyle, Uncle Ho's stilt house has become a symbol of Ho Chi Minh's style and morality, leaving a deep impression in the tens of millions of hearts that have ever visited this place.

As an architectural complex located in the Presidential Palace, belonging to Ba Dinh political center - Ba Dinh district, Hanoi, this is a special relic area associated with Uncle Ho until the last years of his life (May 17, 1958 - February 9, 1969) and an attraction associated with Ho Chi Minh Mausoleum.

❖ **Entrance Fee:** Free

❖ **Address :** 01 Bach Thao, Ngoc Ho, Ba Dinh, Hanoi.

4. One Pillar Pagoda (Chua Mot Cot)

The special thing is that the entire Pagoda is placed on a stone pillar. The upper body has 8 wooden wings that look like a blooming lotus. One Pillar Pagoda is located right next to the vestige complex of Ba Dinh Square - Mausoleum of the President in the center of Ba Dinh district, Hanoi.

The original Pagoda was built under the order of King Ly Thai Tong, the emperor reigned from 1028 to 1054. Although it was destroyed by the French colonialists when withdrawing from the city, it was later completely rebuilt in 1955 and became the most iconic Pagoda in Hanoi.

In 2012, the One Pillar Pagoda was set the record by the Asian Record Organization as "The Pagoda with the most unique architecture".

❖ **Entrance Fee:** Free

❖ **Address :** Ong Ich Khiem, Ba Dinh, Hanoi.

5. Presidential Palace

Hanoi's former Presidential Palace has an elegant exterior and classic French décor.

Designed and completed by architect Auguste Henri Vildieu in 1906, the magnificent Presidential Palace was originally built for the Governor-General of Indochina. After the French colonialist withdrew from Vietnam in 1954, revolutionary leader Ho Chi Minh lived there until his death in 1969. The mansion is only used as a place to welcome officials and organize the State events. visitors could not go inside the Presidential Palace to visit. However, you can learn about the peaceful campus and the famous stilt house of President Ho Chi Minh.

❖ **Entrance Fee:** Free

❖**Address :** 02 Hung Vuong Street, Dien Ban, Ba Dinh, Hanoi.

6. Ho chi minh museum

❖ **Opening :**

+ From 8:00 - 12:0 AM; 2:00 - 4:30 PM (Tue - Thurs, Sat- Sun).

+ From 8:30 - 12:00 AM (Mon and Fri).

❖ **Entrance Fee:** 40.000VND/person (Foreigner).

❖ **Address :** 19 ngach 158/19 Ngoc Ha, Doi Can, Ba Dinh, Hanoi.

❖ **About the museum:**

Ho Chi Minh Museum is a commemorative cultural monument of President Ho Chi Minh with main exhibits about his life and career. The museum is a place where you can learn details about his life and historical role in the struggle for independence of the Vietnamese people.

The museum building itself is an excellent structure. Besides the museum function, the building is also a memorial. The author of this museum is a famous Russian architect and the building bears the imprint of Soviet architectural style.

The museum displays thousands of documents, correspondence and various relics on his years of tireless dedication to the struggle for national independence. The materials are displayed chronologically about the life of him from his childhood, the period of study in France and then the days of fighting along the Communist way.

With the huge and unique information, many visitors have commented that the time to visit the museum is a very profound and memorable experience.

And finally, you can end your visit at the souvenir shop with many art products from famous Vietnamese artists.

Hoa Lo Prison Museum - Maison Centrale

❖ **Opening :** From 8:00 - 12:0 AM; 2:00 - 5:00 PM

❖ **Entrance Fee:** 40.000VND/person (Foreigner).

❖ **Address :** 01 Hoa Lo, Tran Hung Dao, Hoan Kiem, Hanoi.

❖ **About the Hoa Lo Prison Museum:**

Hoa Lo Prison, also known as the Maison Centrale, played an important role in the expansion of French colonial exploitation in Vietnam. Many Vietnamese political prisoners have been tortured and killed here. Later, during the American War, the people of North Vietnam used this place to detain American soldiers.

During the French colonial period, Hoa Lo prison was designed and built with a structure consisting of 4m high stone walls, 0.5m thick reinforced with electric wires. The entire prison area is divided into 4 areas: A, B, C, D, in which:

+ Zone A, B: for prisoners under investigation, non-critical offenders or violate prison's discipline.

+ Zone C: for French or foreign prisoners.

+ Zone D: for prisoners who are awaiting the death penalty.

Dubbed the "hell on earth", the most feared prison in Southeast Asia. During its operation, Hoa Lo Prison has become a place to hold generations of soldiers and activists Viet Nam's revolution. With the prison architecture designed with extremely cruel forms of torture, the most typical of which is a guillotine, the machine has put this prison in the top 10 most famous prisons in the world.

Many revolutionary leaders of Vietnam were detained here, including five persons who later became General Secretary of the Communist Party: Do Muoi, Nguyen Van Cu, Truong Chinh, Le Duan and Nguyen Van Linh. US Senator John McCain was a pilot captured during the Vietnam War and imprisoned for 5 years here. Douglas Peterson, who spent 6 years in prison, became the first ambassador to Vietnam after the war in 1997.

In the prison, you will see the gruesome iron shackles and many artifacts and photos of Vietnamese prisoners wearing wooden straps and shackles on their feet so they cannot stand or move. Prisoners are often starved, tortured, beaten and isolated. Read a quote from a warden saying "dying is easy but life is difficult".

During the Vietnam War, American soldiers sarcastically called the prison "Hanoi Hilton."

Museums of Vietnam (Hanoi)

1. Vietnamese Women's Museum

❖ **Opening :** From 8:00 - 12:0 AM; 2:00 - 4:30 PM (every day except Monday)

❖ **Entrance Fee:** 30.000VND/person

❖ **Address :** 36 Ly Thuong Kiet, Hoan Kiem, Hanoi

Women rule the world. That was how I saw the world before I first stepped out of our home. As a child, I was disoriented and quite shocked to learn in school about the struggles that women have faced over time. In our home, women make the rules. My mother was the breadwinner, and she always had the last say on anything. My dad would make decisions sometimes, but he would always need the approval of my mother. My sister was intimidating; she outperformed my brother in almost anything. They painted my very first picture of women, and it was a pretty powerful tandem.

Apparently, the same could not be said for all families. The female lot had endured many a pain — discrimination, on top of the heap. Still, women have proven time and time again that this world is theirs, too, and they are just as capable in doing the things that men could.

In Hanoi, the significance and accomplishments of the women of Vietnam are enshrined in a museum. The Vietnamese Women's Museum was established by the government and the Women's Union of Vietnam in 1987 to showcase artifacts and documents that highlight the contributions of women in culture, politics, and nation building.

The Vietnam Women's Museum delivers a beautifully presented tribute to the women of Vietnam across the ages. There are plenty of historical contexts alongside a wealth of information on today's more modern Vietnamese woman.

Inside the museum there is lots of narrative as women of the rice paddy fields, service workers, street vendors, female business leaders, academics and mothers are all well represented. Additionally there is plenty of information on everyday life including marriage, family life, fashion and life changing rituals. Interestingly, there are also exhibits on the part women played in Vietnam's wars.

In addition to the permanent displays, there are also regular special exhibitions at the museum which often tackle hard-hitting contemporary women's issues such as human trafficking.

2. Fine Arts Museum of Vietnam

❖ **Opening :** From 8:00 - 12:0 AM; 2:00 - 4:30 PM (every day except Monday)

❖ **Entrance Fee:** 30.000VND/person

❖ **Address :** 66 Nguyen Thai Hoc, Dong Da, Hanoi

The Vietnam Fine Arts Museum has one of the best and most diverse art collections in Vietnam, and a visit here will provide some good insight into Vietnamese culture and history.

The museum is set in a stunning three-storey, 1930s. After a renovation in the 1960s, some traditional architectural elements of Vietnamese communal houses were added, the museum was opened in 1966.

Some 3,000 permanent exhibits are on display, including sculptures, paintings and lacquer works, arranged chronologically from bottom to top. While some information is provided in English, to get a real sense of the meaning of the works and how they relate to Vietnamese history.

artifacts are on permanent display with the following main topics:

- Prehistoric art

- Fine arts from the 11th to the 19th centuries

- Fine arts from the 20th century to the present

- Traditional applied arts

- Folk art

- Vietnamese art pottery from the 11th to 20th centuries, including samples of pottery recovered from 5 ancient ships.

The Museum is a place for contemplating great works of art produced by generations of artists whose life and work reflect the country's major artistic achievements and historical landmarks of the 20th century.

3. Vietnam Military History Museum

❖ **Opening :** From 8:00 - 12:0 AM; 2:00 - 4:30 PM (every day except Monday, Friday)

❖ **Entrance Fee:** 30.000VND/person

❖ **Address :** 28 Dien Bien Phu, Ba Dinh, Hanoi

Vietnam Military History Museum is also known as Military Museum, inaugurated in 1959 on the occasion of 15 years of Vietnamese Military Day, this is one of the oldest museums in Hanoi and is particularly interesting for those wishing to learn about Vietnam military history, because most of the country's history is about war and fighting for independence. There are both indoors and outdoors sections with display of military-related artifacts. Its exhibition dated back to as early as Hung Vuong Era, which is considered as the start of Vietnam as a country, the first thousand year of being colonized by Chinese, as well as the century struggle against French colony.

For more than 50 years of establishment and development, the Vietnam Military History Museum is one of seven national museums and the top of Military museum system of Vietnam. Until now, the warehouse of this museum contains up to more than 150,000 objects on display with precious values in term of history, culture, science, which are preserved in the area of 7,200 m2. The outdoor exhibition area may be the most attractive place because it keeps the huge evidences of the war like: a Soviet-built MiG-21 jet fighter, triumphant amid the wreckage of French aircraft downed at Dien Bien Phu, and a US F-111..

The Vietnam Military History Museum really becomes the center of culture, history, attracting destination for travelers to visit and understand more about the proud Vietnamese military history.

4. Museum of Vietnamese Revolution

❖ **Opening :** From 8:00 - 11:30 AM; 1:30 - 4:00 PM (every day except Monday)

❖ **Entrance Fee:** 40.000VND/person

❖ **Address :** 25 Tong Dan St, Hoan Kiem, Hanoi

❖ **Introduction:**

Unsurprisingly, Vietnam takes its revolutionary foundations very much to heart. They're shown off and commemorated in the national Museum of the Vietnamese Museum in downtown Hanoi.

Established in 1959 and apparently only infrequently updated since, the museum is a charming clash of ideas and history. It's housed in a yellow colonial-style building that once served as the Trade Department Building in the Tong Dan area, just a block from Hanoi's opera house. Its wide, tiled corridors are right out of 1950s Western government bureaucracy. Glass showcases have everything from weapons and flags used by revolutionaries on the front lines to propaganda posters to the everyday utensils used by Vietnamese peasants. There are statues of Ho Chi Minh the scholar, Ho Chi Minh the statesmen, and various other revolutionary leaders like Tran Phy.

The Museum of Vietnamese Revolution will be a worthwhile stop if you're starting your travels in Hanoi or if you have a particular fascination with museums and Vietnam's revolutionary history. There are ample more interesting opportunities to engage with the country's revolutionary war history elsewhere - including reading a good book.

❖ Division of Sections:

There are 29 rooms with the content of 3 main parts.

Part 1: From room 1 – 9: The French colonialism (1858 – 1945) - the struggle of Vietnamese people for independence.

Part 2: From room 10 – 24: The Vietnam War period (1945 – 1975) – the revolution against the invaders to protect the sovereignty of the country.

Part 3: From room 25 - 27: The Post-war period (1975 – now) – Vietnam on its road toward a socialist democratic and fair society.

Moreover, with the respect to Ho Chi Minh President, room 28 and 29 are places to exhibit the gifts collection of people from all over the world dedicating "Uncle Ho" as well as Vietnamese Communist Party.

5. National Museum of Vietnamese History

❖ **Opening :** From 8:00 - 12:0 AM; 2:00 - 5:00 PM (every day except Monday)

❖ **Entrance Fee:** 40.000VND/person ~ $1.6

❖ **Address:** 01 Trang Tien, Hoan Kiem, Hanoi

Vietnam National Museum of History Hanoi is home to rich and diverse collections of historical relics and thematic exhibitions on Vietnamese culture and history. The museum gives visitors a broad overview of the development of Vietnam from the prehistoric period through the national formation period, a very thorough and comprehensive historical outlook that other museums cannot offer.

❖ **Introduction**

4.000 square meters in space, the museum is now housing over 200.000 objects and materials which are relics of Vietnamese history flowing from prehistoric to present. Housed in a colonial French building which is a cupola-shaped edifice, the museum was designed as a combination of French and Chinese architecture. The building designed by Hebrard, an eminent French architect, and urban planner, incorporates double walls and balconies for a natural airing system and protection from sunshine.

In particular, strongly impressing tourists when visiting the 1st floor of museum is 7 bronze drums: Dong Son bronze drum, Ngoc Lu bronze drum, Nong Cong bronze drum or Thanh Vinh bronze drum... placed around the large pillar carved crane and ancient Vietnamese people, the famous cultural icons in Vietnam. Keeping moving into the museum, you will catch the space displaying precious objects of religious works from Tran Dynasty and historical relics, materials, architectural ornaments and pictures of the famous relics, namely Pho Minh Pagoda and Tower (Nam Dinh province), Kiep Bac Temple (Hai Duong province), Binh Son Tower (Vinh Phuc province)...

The museum also houses two fixed thematic galleries: Champa stone artistic carvings and Oc Eo culture - Phu Nam. The Champa stone collection is presented in an open space in the 2nd floor hallway of octagonal-shaped room looking down the hall of the museum. The collections are introduced in chronology stretching from the 7th to 13th century with more than 50 specimens collected from the provinces in Vietnam such as Quang Binh, Quang Nam, Binh Dinh... The journey of exploring Hanoi travel will be definitely much more impressive when you set foot on the museum.

National Museum of Vietnamese History is home to keep and display the precious tangible cultural heritages of the country. It introduces Vietnamese history through rare and precious artifacts helping you understand the long-lasting cultural history as well as the process of building and defending Vietnam nation. These collections, thematic galleries of Vietnam history contribute to bring the museum to become one of the most fascinating museums in Hanoi. Thanks to its unique values, National Museum of Vietnamese History displays its significant contributions in promoting the image of Hanoi tourism closer to tourists both at home and abroad.

Temple of Literature (Van Mieu Quoc Tu Giam)

❖ **Opening :** From 8:00 - 12:0 AM; 2:00 - 5:00 PM

❖ **Entrance Fee:** 30.000VND/person ~ $1.25

❖ **Address:** 58 Quoc Tu Giam, Van Mieu, Dong Da, Hanoi

About 2km west of Sword Lake, the Temple of Literature is a very first stop-over point of any tourists when they come to Hanoi. It is a rare example of well-preserved traditional Vietnamese architecture as well as Hanoians' spirit of study in the past.

❖ **History of Temple of Literature**

Founded in 1070 by Emperor Ly Thanh Tong, the complex was originally dedicated to honor Confucius (Khong Tu). After that, it became Vietnam's Imperial Academy – a prestigious school for top academics. Students began enrolling at the Imperial Academy in 1076. Once accepted, students took 3 to 7 years to complete the curriculum, which is undoubtedly influenced by Chinese literature, poetry and history. Scholars had the opportunity to sit the National Exam after completion and continue to Royal Exam (which is administered by the Emperor himself). Obviously, attending such a prestigious academy is a high honor, especially some of the most brilliant minds in Vietnamese history graduated from the prestigious academy. Before 1442, University admission was exclusive for Royal and noble families. After that, under the reign of King Tran Thai Tong, Quoc Tu Giam was renamed Quoc Hoc Vien, and take on the children of civilians with excellent academic ability.

❖ Architecture

Temple of literature complex encompasses five walled courtyards connected by gateways. The number of courtyards, five, is the symbolic number of five basic elements forming the world:

♦ Five basic elements: Metal – Wood – Fire – Water – The earth.

Phoenix and dragon symbols are used to represent the Empress and Emperor:

♦ A phoenix represents beauty – A dragon represents power.

1/ The First Courtyard- Dai Trung Mon (The great middle gate)

The first courtyard extends from Dai Trung Mon (The Great Middle Gate) to the Dai Trung area.

Dai Trung Mon is a combination of the names of two great books of Confucianism:

♦ Dai Hoc (Great learning)

♦ Trung Dung (The Doctrine of the Mean)

Two smaller gates on the left and right side of Dai Trung Môn

♦ Accomplished Virtue (Thanh Duc)

♦ Attained Talent (Dat Tai)

In ancient Orient concept, left side is more important than right (From Confucius point of view). Therefore, Virtue is more important than Talent.

The carp symbol located at the top of the gate has a meaningful story due to Chinese legendary: "Many carps swim upstream against the river's strong current in a contest held by God, but only few are capable of the final leap over the waterfall. If a carp successfully makes the jump, it can transform into a powerful dragon."

♦ The carp overcoming waterfall: hardships that students must overcome if they want to get success in education.

♦ The carp becoming dragon: student's promotion in social rank.

2/ The Second Courtyard- Khue Van Cac (The Pavilion of Constellation)

Located in the Second Courtyard is Khue Van Pavilion (Pavilion of Constellation)

♦ A unique architectural work was built in 1805 under Nguyễn Dynasty- regarded as the symbol of Hanoi in the present time.

♦ Given the meaning of term 'Constellation' as the brightest star – that carry the wish for development and prosperity for education and culture of Vietnam.

On top of the pavilion is the combination of the circle and the square:

♦ The circle represents the sky

♦ The square represents the earth.

This is the symbol of the yin and yang harmony.

3/ The Third Courtyard – Thien Quang well and Doctor Stelae

Thien Quang Well

In the center of the third courtyard is Thien Quang well (Well of Heavenly Clarity). Some functions of Thien Quang Well are:

♦ To keep the atmosphere of Văn Miếu complex to be tranquil

♦ To purify people's mind

♦ Being as a mirror for people to arranging their dress before entering the most sacred part of the complex.

Doctor Steles

A general Doctor Stele includes 3 parts:

♦ The first part wrote nice words toward the Emperor, his royal court and Confucianism

♦ The second part commented on the importance of building steles and the responsibility of successful people toward the country

♦ The third part was information about the exams and successful students

Originally, there are 91 doctorate steles.

However due to wars and natural disaster, there are only 82 left.

In putting the steles on the back of the tortoises:

♦ The tortoises stand for longevity and wisdom so the names of successful students would last forever.

4. The Fourth Courtyard- Dai Thanh Mon (The gate to great success), and Dai Bai Duong (House of Ceremony)

Leading to the Fourth Courtyard of the temple is Đại Thành Môn (The Gate to the Great Success)

In the center of the fourth courtyard is the Đại Bái Đường (House of Ceremony)

♦ The house of ceremony is a place for Emperors and Fellows to make their offerings to Confucius. New doctors come to House of Ceremony to kneel and bow to show their respect

In Dai Bai Duong, the pair of crane and turtle that present desire of longevity and eternity.

49

5. The Fifth Courtyard, grounds of the Imperial Academy

The Fifth Courtyard has been through long history.

♦ In 1076, Emperor Ly Nhan Tong ordered the construction of an imperial academy as a fifth courtyard

♦ In 1946, the courtyard was destroyed by the French.

♦ In 2000, it was reconstructed on the ground of the original "Imperial Academy" as a temple.

The upper floor is dedicated to the three emperors who contributed mostly to the foundation of the temple and the academy:

♦ Ly Thanh Tong (1023–1072), who founded the temple in 1070 (In the middle of altar)

♦ Ly Nhan Tong (1066–1127), who founded the Imperial Academy (On the right altar)

♦ Le Thanh Tong (1442–1497), who ordered the built of doctor statues in 1484 (on the left altar)

Around the Fifth Courtyard, some buildings hold a drum and a bronze bell. The drum is 2.01 metres wide, 2.65 metres high, has a volume of 10 m3 and weighs 700 kilograms. The bell was cast in 2000. It has a height of 2.1 metres and it is 0.99 meters wide.

❖ **Note:**

As Temple of Literature is a formal historical site, visitors should pay serious attention to the dress code as visitors need to be respectable.

In detail, no hat, shorts, mini skirt or tank-top…when being in worshipping/sanctuary area.

Visitors should not rub the turtle's head, write, draw, stand or sit on the stele.

Hanoi Opera House

❖ **Opening :** From 8:00 - 12:0 AM; 2:00 - 5:00 PM

❖ **Entrance Fee:**

+ 400.000VND/person (Visiting combining art performances)

+ 120.000VND/person (Just visiting)

❖ **Address:** 01 Trang Tien, Hoan Kiem, Hanoi

❖ **About the Hanoi Opera House:**

Located in the French Quarter, Hanoi Opera House is not only a historical, artistic building but also a home to classical art lovers.

Visitors can admire the magnificent architecture of Hanoi Opera House or buy tickets to see one of the regular shows held to see the magnificent interior of the theater.

The French colonial government built the theater in the first decade of the 20th century. This Renaissance-style building was built in the archetype of the Palace of Garnie - one of the two famous opera houses of Paris - and is one of the city's most famous architectural landmarks. The theater is still active and is the venue for performances of many famous Vietnamese and foreign singers and artists.

Opera House has historical and architectural values that are very important in the cultural life of Hanoi people. In the first phase after Independence Day, the theater was the venue for the National Assembly meetings of the Democratic Republic of Vietnam. Meanwhile, the square area around the theater used to be fierce battlefields between the Viet Minh and the French and Japanese armies.

Come during the day to admire the theater's typical colonial architecture. Walk around the immense garden yard in front of the theater to see all the corners of this grand, imposing architecture with Gothic and neoclassical architecture.

Today, Hanoi Opera House hosts both classical French and Italian opera and Vietnamese plays. And of course, it is indispensable for ballet shows or programs of traditional art troupes at the theater to accommodate 600 seats. If you If you are an art lover, this is a place you can't be missed, but remember to plan early as tickets for art shows here often sell well.

St Joseph Cathedral Hanoi

❖ **Opening :** For inside visit: visitors can only enter St. Joseph's Cathedral in Hanoi in the opening time of ceremonial practice as the following schedule:

Weekday: 5.30am and 6.15 pm.

Saturday: 6:00pm.

Sunday: 5:00am, 7:00am, 9:00am, 11:00am, 4:00pm, 6:00pm, and 8:00pm.

A special ceremony is on March 19th every year.

❖ **Entrance Fee:** Free

❖ **Address:** No.40 Nha Chung street, Hoan Kiem, Hanoi.

❖ **History:**

In 1882, after the French army conquered Hanoi, the cathedral was constructed and completed in 1886. The cathedral and Nha Chung area were built on the land formerly belonging to Bao Thien pagoda, which was built under Ly dynasty.

The architecture with domes of the cathedral follows the Gothic style and design of Paris Cathedral. It is 64.5m in length, 20.5m in width with two bell towers of 31.5m-height. Though the appearance of the cathedral, from the doors, the colorful window glass, to the religious paintings for decoration follows Western style, the main interior part is decorated in Vietnamese way with two typical colors yellow and red. Outside, in front of the cathedral is the statue of Mother Maria.

❖ **Architecture:**

One of the architectural features of the cathedral in Hanoi is designed in the Gothic style and simulated from the church of Notre Dame de Paris. Thus, the church has the interference of the East with the West, between Buddhism and Christianity.

The center of the square in front of the church is the St Mary of the Metal Hall, surrounded by flower baskets, palanquins and a rocky cave behind it to enhance the landscape.

When viewed from outside, the cathedral of Hanoi brings majestic and ancient beauty with old mossy lime on the wall that has soaked the color of time. However, when you step inside, visitors will be able to observe the magnificent and modern architecture.

The Hanoi Cathedral is divided into three sections from the entrance including the reception hall with over posts for choirs and musicians; Space for lay people and sanctuary to celebrate Mass.

Visitors can only visit the church on a one-day tours in Hanoi by the side gate, where most of the windows are colored with stained glass depicting religious themes bearing European architecture. There are many decorative objects, motifs along the aisles, on the altar and in the traditional Vietnamese style.

Come to Hanoi Cathedral - one of the beautiful tourist in Hanoi, you will be immersed in the space of architecture is extremely beautiful, fanciful and full of light.

In particular, there is a chance to admire the statue of St. Joseph higher than 2m and made of terracotta in the main hall. Besides, if you wander around Nha Chung Street in the early winter or walk the streets of the night. You will feel like you are lost in the classic European sky and luxury.

If you are planning to go to Hanoi Cathedral. Do not forget to check out the Saint Joseph Cathedral Hanoi Mass Schedule as well as share useful to have the most complete and memorable tours in Hanoi from Vietnam Travel Guide 2019.

West lake

As one of the capital's most beautiful and famous sights, West Lake has an exotic charm and charm. Here, you can admire the romantic beauty of an ancient Hanoi, where associated with many ups and downs of history, memories of the people of Hanoi.

With an area of over 500ha and an 18km circumference, West Lake is the largest natural lake in Hanoi's inner city. Considered as the "green lung" of Hanoi, West Lake always brings cool breeze, making people's minds feel strange.

Around the West Lake, There are many ancient Pagodas and structures. These place are not only spiritual places but also places to preserve the historical and cultural values of Hanoi, such as: Van Nien Pagoda, Thien Nien Pagoda, Vong Thi Pagoda, Quan Thanh Temple, Tran Quoc Pagoda ...

Besides, you will also enjoy famous dishes around the west lake such as shrimp cakes, rice vermicelli, coconut Ice cream ... Or participate in leisure activities such as cycling around the west lake, boating west lake ....

Imperial Citadel of Thang Long

❖ Opening Hours: Tuesday – Sunday 08:00am – 11:30am ; 02:00pm – 5:00pm

❖ Location: 19C Hoang Dieu, Dien Ban, Ba Dinh, Hanoi

❖ Price Range: VND 30,000

The Imperial Citadel of Thang Long, is an intriguing relic of Vietnam's history and, signifying its historical and cultural importance, was made a UNESCO World Heritage Site in 2010. Also known as the Hanoi Citadel, many artefacts and items dating back to between the 6th and 20th centuries were excavated in 2004, including foundations of old palaces, ancient roads, ponds and wells.

The ancient site was the political centre of the country for 13 consecutive centuries and served as the capital of Vietnam for eight centuries. A notable attraction in the Imperial Citadel of Thang Long was the Hanoi Flag Tower, a renovated 40-metre-tall stone fortress offering expansive views of Ba Dinh Square and Hanoi City Centre.

Old Quarter Area

Hanoi Old Quarter is located in the West and North of Hoan Kiem Lake including 36 streets, each street concentrates on selling a different item. The limit of the old town north to Hang Dau street, the west is Phung Hung street, the south is the streets: Hang Bong, Hang Gai, Cau Go and Hang Thung, the east is Tran Quang Khai and Tran Nhat Duat.

For a feel of rich old Vietnamese customs, you can also stroll along ancient commercial streets surrounding Hoan Kiem Lake dating back about 1,000 years. Hanoi Old Quarter's most popular attractions comprise mostly quaint Buddhist shrines, street markets, and traditional Vietnamese arts.

Come on, let's find out!

Hoan Kiem Lake & Turtle Tower

Hoan Kiem Lake

This legend is really interesting. Close your eyes and turn back time to the Le Dynasty 6 centuries ago to witness the legendary story. During the war against the Minh aggressors, King Le Thai To was given a precious fairy Sword by the Golden Turtle God. After 10 years of continuous struggling, the King finally defeated the Chinese and reclaimed the nation's independence. After that, on a nice day, while boating on lake Luc Thuy, a large turtle came towards him.

It immediately grabbed the sword with its mouth and submerged. The king mourned lost of such a valuable sword, yet could not find either the turtle or the sword. He realized that the God must have lent him the sword to drive back the enemy, but then that his nation was free, the sword must be returned. Hence, King Le Thai To named the lake Ho Hoan Kiem.

From past to present, people have never seen Sword Lake run out of water. The water in the lake is natural water, relatively stable and it is not clear where the water comes from. To this day, scientists have not yet explained this "mystery". In addition, year-round the lake of Sword Lake always has a charming green color.

Dubbed as the heart of Hanoi capital, Hoan Kiem Lake has a central location in Hanoi capital, so you can get here easily by personal or public transportation.

Turtle Tower

Located in the middle of Hoan Kiem Lake, the Turtle Tower has long been a familiar image to the people of Hanoi in particular and Vietnamese people in general. According to historical records, the name Turtle Tower is because the tower was built on the island of turtles - small mounds of land rise in the middle of the lake, where Ho Guom turtles often go to the sun or lay eggs.

Tower architecture is an intersection of European gothic architecture combined with the curved roof of Vietnamese architecture, the turtle tower has created a unique, distinctive beauty and has become a close symbol of Hanoi capital.

Ngoc Son Temple

❖ **Opening :** From 7:00 - 12:0 AM; 1:30 - 6:00 PM

❖ **Entrance Fee:** 30.000VND ~ $1.25

❖ **Address:** Dinh Tien Hoang, Hang Trong, Hoan Kiem, Hanoi.

Den Ngoc Son, or the Temple of the Jade Mountain is one of Hanoi's most picturesque temples. It is built on an islet in Ho Hoan Kiem where, in the 16th-18th centuries, there was a country villa used by the Trinh mandarins when they boated on the lake. In the 19th century, the site became a Buddhist pagoda, then a temple for the cult of a deified Chinese warrior, Quan Cong, and later for the Spirits of Literature and of the Soil. This shrine is now dedicated to Tran Hung Dao, a 13th century Vietnamese military national hero, scholar Van Xuong, and to Nguyen Van Sieu, a Confucian master who assumed responsibility for extensive additions and repairs made to the temple and the surrounding areas from 1864. The present building reflects the Chinese style favored by the Nguyen rulers of that time.

To get to the temple, the visitor walks through the Three-Passage Gate (Tam Quan) and across the Morning Sunlight Bridge (The Huc). The entrance complex, designed by Nguyen Van Sieu, consists of a series of three gates, replete with Taoist symbolism.

The first gate displays a series of parallel sentences. The two large red Chinese characters on the first gate are Happiness on the right, and Prosperity on the left. Conditions of a good life, very important to Vietnamese, are Happiness (Phuc), Prosperity (Loc) and Long Life (Tho).

Just inside the first gate is the Pen Tower (Thap But), a ten-meter high stone structure whose tip resembles a writing brush, standing on a "mountain" in the shape of a peach, known as the Writing Pad (Dai Nghien). The mountain represents a good foundation, or the earth, and the symbols on the tower say "Writing on the clear blue sky" (meaning always be truthful). This is a principle of feng shui, the Taoist philosophy of the harmonious arrangement of elements. The Pen Tower is the introduction to the temple dedicated to literature and poetry. There is a small altar on the mountain where one can pray to receive permission to enter the temple.

The second gate is surrounded by Taoist symbols. On the left is the tiger. On the right is the Vietnamese dragon. The tiger and the dragon are the symbols of stability for a large construction, following the feng shui theory. Panels on the reverse of the gate show the carp gazing at the moon's reflection, and a pine tree with roosting storks (phoenix), which symbolizes longevity.

Above the third gate is a large stone representing an ink stone or inkpot. Nguyen Van Sieu placed this stone so that on the 5th of May (lunar calendar) the shadow of the Pen Tower falls on the ink stone. Why this date? There are 120 stars in the Chinese/Vietnamese Taoist horoscope. One of these is represented by Van Xuong, the saint responsible for literature. On May 5, Van Xuong's star crosses the sun's trajectory.

Thang Long Puppet Theater

❖ **Opening :** Daily 3:00 pm, 4:10 pm, 5:20 pm, 6:30 pm & 10:00 pm

❖ **Entrance Fee:** 100.000VND ~ $4.34

❖ **Address:** 57B, Dinh Tien Hoang Street, Hoan Kiem District, Hanoi

The world-famous Thang Long Water Puppet Theatre in Hanoi has its roots in an art form that dates back to the 11th century. The tradition of water puppet theatre stems from a time when rice paddy fields were flooded and villagers would make entertainment by standing in the waist-deep water with the puppets performing over the water. Using large rods to support the puppets it appeared as if they were moving across the water with the puppeteers hidden behind a screen.

This tradition is unique to North Vietnam but has recently found fame on stages all over the world.

Today's performances usually include a number of short sketches rather than one long story, taking the audience on a journey of ancient village life, agricultural harvests and dances of mythical creatures.

This is definitely an activity that you cannot ignore when visiting the old town area.

Dong Xuan Market

❖ **Opening :** Daily 6:00 am - 7:00 pm

❖ **Address:** Dong Xuat Street, Hoan Kiem District, Hanoi

Established in 1889, Dong Xuan Market is housed within a four-storey Soviet-style building on the northern edge of Hanoi Old Quarter. It's also known as Hanoi's largest indoor market, offering a wide range of goods such as fresh produce, souvenirs, accessories and clothing, as well as electronic and household appliances. Similar to most markets in Southeast Asia, Dong Xuan Market has a bustling wet market section on the ground floor, where locals shop for seafood, meat, and vegetables while the back section sells an array of pets (cats, dogs, and fish) and fresh flowers from all across Vietnam. If you're looking to shop for souvenirs, head to the upper levels, where you can find numerous stalls selling tee shirts, fabrics, school uniforms, handbags, handicrafts, all of which are sold at wholesale prices.

There's also a massive dining area within Dong Xuan Market, with food vendors selling Vietnamese coffee and exotic local dishes for as low as VND 15,000. Surrounding Dong Xuan Market are many more shops where you can purchase traditional Dong Ho drawings, Bat Trang ceramics, Binh Da embroideries and laces, and sand paintings. Within walking distance of Hoan Kiem Lake, Dong Xuan Market is a must-visit if you're looking to experience the local lifestyle (you might even end up leaving with a pair of cheap sunglasses and a Vietnamese conical hat).

Bach Ma Temple

❖ **Opening :** Daily 7:00 am - 5:00 pm

❖ **Address:** 76 Hang Buom, Hoan Kiem District, Hanoi

Bach Ma Temple is believed to be the oldest temple in Hanoi. This Buddhist temple was originally built in the ninth century by King Ly Thai To to honour a white horse that guided him to this site, where he chose to construct his city walls. The temple was moved to its current location in the Old Quarter of Hanoi in the 18th century, during the Ly Dynasty, to guard the east side of Thang Long.

You enter the temple through some ancient wooden doors after which you will be able to see the beautiful decorated interior and a red-lacquered funeral palanquin. Inside the temple you will find a statue of the white horse, a shrine to Confucius and a Phoenix Altar for offerings to the four seasons. Bach Ma Temple is still actively used by worshippers who come there to burn incense and pray.

Heritage House

❖ **Opening :** Daily 7:00 am - 5:00 pm

❖ **Address:** 87 Ma May, Hang Buom, Hoan Kiem District, Hanoi

As one of the attractive places to visit in the old town and also one of the Old Quarter's best-restored properties, the old house in 87 Ma May is a traditional house that recreates the living space, the characteristic of the ancient Hanoi people. The house is open regularly for tourists to visit, the entrance fee is 10,000 VND.

There are crafts and trinkets for sale here, including silver jewellery, basketwork and Vietnamese tea sets, and there's usually a calligrapher or other craftsperson at work too.

Hanoi Ceramic Mosaic Mural

Spanning almost 4km along the Song Hong dyke, from its terminus at the Long Bien Bridge, this mural project holds the Guinness World Record for being the largest ceramic mosaic on the planet. The colourful mural lines busy roads, uses ceramics produced at nearby Bat Trang and depicts different periods in Vietnam's history. Both local and international artists commenced work on the project in 2007, completed in 2010 for Hanoi's 1000th-birthday celebrations.

Long Bien Bridge

A symbol of the tenacity and resilience of the Hanoian people, the Long Bien Bridge (built between 1898 and 1902).

The bridge was formerly named Paul Doumer by the French, but Vietnamese have called it Long Bien. It was the first steel bridge across Red river in Hanoi, and one of four greatest bridges in the world at the time it was built.

More than 100 years with decades of war, Long Bien Bridge was bombed many times by air attacks by American army in 1967, 1972; and many spans of the bridge were destroyed. The left spans still remaining today remind us of an unforgettable past. The bridge, hence, is not only a traffic construction, a nice architecture, but also a living historical relic.

If you have a chance to visit Hanoi, do not forget to take a walk on Long Bien Bridge for sightseeing, feeling the daily life of Hanoians, and enjoying peaceful moments at the present but not forgetting memorable past.

My Dinh National Stadium

My Dinh National Stadium is the second largest national stadium in Vietnam (after Can Tho Stadium). It takes place big matches, attracting thousands of fans.

My Dinh Stadium is designed with 4 stands (A, B, C, D) in which stands A and B with a 2-storey roof design. Stands C and D are designed with 1 floor and no roof. The main side of the yard is 105 meters wide by 68 meters.

With 419 function rooms, 337 lights arranged in 4 different 54m high columns, My Dinh National Stadium can accommodate more than 40,000 seats.

If you are a football lover and lucky to visit Hanoi at the time of the football matches of the Vietnamese team, you will be extremely surprised by the enthusiasm of the Vietnamese fans.

Chapter 5: Hanoi cuisine & Street food

Pho, types of noodle

1. Pho Hanoi

Since the 1930s, Pho has become a familiar dish in the life of the people. On the narrow old streets of Hanoi in the past, it is not difficult to see pho shops selling from dawn till late, fragrant typical of traditional Pho.

Throughout the centuries, this long-standing dish is still preserved and transmitted through generations of Hanoians. Pho is a specialty not only of the capital but also a Vietnamese culinary brand.

Nowadays, it is very easy to find a Pho restaurant in Hanoi, but the traditional pho restaurant retains the essence of old Pho not everyone knows.

You can enjoy chicken or beef noodle soup, each dish has a unique flavor.

Top most delicious pho in Hanoi

❖ Pho Gia Truyen Bat Dan

Address: 49 Bat Dan, Cua Dong, Hoan Kiem, Hanoi

Open: 7:00am - 8:00pm

Prices: VND35,000 - 55,000 ~ $1.20 - $2.50

❖ Pho Thin Lo Duc

Address: 13 Lo Duc, Ngo Thi Nham, Hai Ba Trung, Hanoi

Open: 6:00am - 9:00pm

Prices: VND40,000 - 60,000 ~ $1.70 - $2.60

❖ Pho 10 Ly Quoc Su

Address: 10 Ly Quoc Su, Hang Trong, Hoan Kiem, Hanoi

Open: 6:00am - 9:30pm

Prices: VND50,000 - 80,000 ~ $2.17 - $3.40

❖ Pho Suong

Address: 36B Mai Hac De, Hai Ba Trung, Hanoi

Open: 6:30am - 9:30 pm

Prices: VND30,000 - 100,000 ~ $1.30 - $4.34

❖ Pho "Bưng" Hang Trong

Address: No 1 Hang Trong, Hoan Kiem, Hanoi

Open: 3:30pm - 8:30 pm

Prices: VND30,000 - 60,000 ~ $1.30 - $2.60

❖ Pho Vui

Address: 25 Hang Giay, Hoan Kiem, Hanoi

Open: 7:00am - 9:30 pm

Prices: VND20,000 - 50,000 ~ $0.87 - $2.17

2. Pho Cuon (Rolled Pho)

Pho - one of the most delicious dishes in the world, this traditional dish is always the pride of Vietnamese ethnic cuisine. For a long time, people have been familiar with dishes such as beef noodle soup, chicken noodle soup ... However, with their creativity, besides the water noodle dishes, Hanoi people have made other variations of pho such as fried pho. Pho, stir-fried Pho, stir-fried Pho … and the most typical is still pho.

The introduction of pho noodle creates new and original features for Vietnamese noodle soup. Pho is frugal, not too picky in processing but still has a very special attraction.

Top most delicious Rolled pho in Hanoi

❖ Pho Cuon Vinh Phong

Address: 40 Ngu Xa, Truc Bach, Ba Dinh, Hanoi

Open: 8:00 am - 10:00 pm

Prices: VND20,000 - 50,000 ~ $0.87 - $2.17

❖ Pho Cuon Huong Mai

Address: 25 Ngu Xa, Truc Bach, Ba Dinh, Hanoi

Open: 9:00 am - 10:00 pm

Prices: VND30,000 - 50,000 ~ $1.3 - $2.17

❖ Pho Cuon Hung Ben

Address: 33 Ngu Xa, Truc Bach, Ba Dinh, Hanoi

Open: 9:00 am - 10:00 pm

Prices: VND20,000 - 50,000 ~ $0.87 - $2.17

❖ Pho Cuon Choén

Address: 156 O Cho Dua, Dong Da, Hanoi

Open: 9:00 am - 10:00 pm

Prices: VND50,000 - 100,000 ~ $2.17 - $4.34

3. Bun Rieu Cua (crab noodle soup)

Perhaps mentioning Hanoi cuisine, people remember pho first, but I have to say that I prefer noodles. Pho may be the quintessence, but bun is actually the creative dish of Hanoi chefs. Bun rieu, bun thang, bun cha, bun oc …. Each noodle dish is a kind of flavor made up of separate recipes, with its own rules and standards.

In the past, "Bun rieu" consisted of finely ground crab cooked with tomatoes, "Bun rieu" now has fried tofu, beef and sometimes even some thin grilled chopped fish.

Top most delicious "Bun Rieu Cua" in Hanoi

❖ Bun Rieu Huyen Thu

Address: 2F Quang Trung, Tran Hung Dao, Hoan Kiem, Hanoi

Open: 6:00 am - 2:00 pm

Prices: VND25,000 - 70,000 ~ $1.08 - $3.04

❖ Bun Rieu 16 Hang Luoc

Address: 16 Hang Luoc, Hoan Kiem, Hanoi

Open: 6:00 am - 9:00 am

Prices: VND25,000 - 35,000 ~ $1.08 - $1.52

❖ Bun Rieu Trang

Address: 23 Nguyen Sieu, Hoan Kiem, Hanoi

Open: 6:00 am - 2:00 pm

Prices: VND30,000 - 50,000 ~ $1.30 - $2.17

❖ Bun Rieu Hang Bac

Address: 11 Hang Bac, Hoan Kiem, Hanoi

Open: 7:00 am - 10:00 pm

Prices: VND25,000 - 45,000 ~ $1.08 - $1.95

❖ Bun Rieu Suon Sun Nguyen Du

Address: 50 Nguyen Du, Hai Ba Trung, Hanoi

Open: 6:30 am - 9:00 pm

Prices: VND30,000 - 40,000 ~ $1.30 - $1.74

4. Bun Thang Hanoi (Hanoi combo noodle soup)

As a sophisticated dish, showing the elegant style of Hanoi cuisine, "Bun Thang" has a perfect combination of color, flavor and taste.

Bun thang has a lot of ingredients, basically noodles, chicken, silk rolls, chicken eggs, shrimp, radishes, shrimp paste, herbs ...

The broth for bun thang must be chicken broth, not pork or beef bones because of the rancid smell. After cooking, the water is sweet, rich, clear and very delicious, "Bun thang" will attract you at first sight.

Top most delicious "Bun Thang" in Hanoi

❖ Bun Thang Ba Duc

Address: 48 Cau Go, Hang Bac, Hoan Kiem, Hanoi

Open: 7:00 am - 10:00 pm

Prices: VND30,000 - 55,000 ~ $1.30 - $2.40

❖ Bun Thang Thuan Ly

Address: 33 Hang Hom, Hang Gai, Hoan Kiem, Hanoi

Open: 6:00 am - 10:00 pm

Prices: VND30,000 - 40,000 ~ $1.30 - $1.74

❖ Bun Thang Hang Hanh

Address: 29 Hang Hanh, Hang Trong, Hoan Kiem, Hanoi

Open: 6:00 am - 9:00 pm

Prices: VND30,000 - 50,000 ~ $1.30 - $2.17

❖ Bun Thang Tu Lun

Address: 22 Hang Trong, Hoan Kiem, Hanoi

Open: 6:00 am - 01:00 pm

Prices: VND25,000 - 40,000 ~ $1.08 - $1.74

❖ Bun Thang Pho Co

Address: 698 Lac Long Quan, Tay Ho, Hanoi

Open: 6:00 am - 02:00 pm

Prices: VND25,000 - 40,000 ~ $1.08 - $1.74

5. Bun Cha (Noodle with grilled pork)

Bun cha is a local dish that originated in Hanoi, the capital of Vietnam. Throughout Vietnam you can find a lot of dishes that share a similar recipe to bun cha (like bun thit nuong in Saigon), however, the dish is unbeatable.

This simple dish is a great combination of savory and fresh flavors, it has a vibrant color and the harmony of the meat and vegetables is incomparable.

On May 23 2016, US President Barack Obama arrived in Vietnam , for his tenth trip to Asia with renowned chef-turned-television host Anthony Bourdain. They dined at local restaurant Bún chả Hương Liên in Hanoi, where they chatted over bowls of grilled pork with noodles and other Vietnamese dishes.

Top most delicious "Bun Cha" in Hanoi

❖ Bun Cha Huong Lien

Address: 24 Le Van Huu, Hai Ba Trung, Hanoi / 59 Lang Ha, Dong Da, Hanoi

Open: 8:00 am - 8:30 pm

Prices: VND40,000 - 60,000 ~ $1.74 - $2.6

❖ Bun Cha Hang Quat

Address: 24 Le Van Huu, Hai Ba Trung, Hanoi / 59 Lang Ha, Dong Da, Hanoi

Open: 10:00 am - 2:00 pm

Prices: VND25,000 - 40,000 ~ $1.08 - $1.74

❖ Bun Cha 74 Hang Quat

Address : 74 Hang Quat, Hang Gai, Hoan Kiem, Hanoi

Open: 10:00 am - 2:00 pm

Prices: VND25,000 - 40,000 ~ $1.08 - $1.74

❖ Bun Cha Cua Dong

Address: 41 Cua Dong, Hoan Kiem, Hanoi

Open: 10:30 am - 9:00 pm

Prices: VND20,000 - 30,000 ~ $0.87 - $1.30

❖ Bun Cha 47C Mai Hac De

Address: 47C Mai Hac De, Bui Thi Xuan, Hai Ba Trung, Hanoi

Open: 10:00 am - 3:00 pm

Prices: VND20,000 - 30,000 ~ $0.87 - $1.30

6. Bun Dau Mam Tom (noodle with fried tofu & shrimp paste)

Referring to the "Bun dau mam tom", you will find in every corner of Hanoi. This is the most rustic sidewalk dish that attracts domestic and international visitors. Therefore, this dish is the first suggestion in the list of delicious dishes to try in Hanoi.

Top most delicious "Bun Dau Mam Tom" in Hanoi

❖ Bun Dau Mam Tom Cay Da - Thuy Khe

Address: 253B Thuy Khe, Tay Ho, Ha Noi

Open: 10:00 am - 9:00 pm

Prices: VND30,000 - 80,000 ~ $1.30 - $3.48

❖ Bun Dau Mam Tom 5

Address: No.6 Ma May, Hang Buom, Hoan Kiem, Hanoi

Open: 10:30 am - 4:30 pm

Prices: VND20,000 - 50,000 ~ $0.87 - $2.17

❖ Bun Dau Mam Tom Co Tuyen

Address: 31 Ngo 29, Hang Khay, Hoan Kiem, Hanoi

Open: 7:00 am - 8:30 pm

Prices: VND40,000 - 200,000 ~ $1.74 - $8.7

❖ Bun Dau Mam Tom Nghia Tan

Address: No.104 C3 Nghia Tan, Cau Giay, Hanoi

Open: 9:00 am - 8:30 pm

Prices: VND20,000 - 40,000 ~ $0.87 - $1.74

7. Bun Oc (Snail vermicelli/ noodle soup)

"Bun Oc" was introduced to the public around the world on Parts Unknown (Channel CNN) - the culinary discovery television show of famous chef Anthony Bourdain - who used to eat "Bun cha Hanoi" with President Barack Obama during the US President's official visit to Vietnam in May 2016.

Similar to "Bun Rieu Cua" , "Bun Oc" is also ranked among the top delicious dishes not to be missed when coming to Hanoi. Anthony Bourdain used two words "magic" to talk about Hanoi snail noodles after enjoying

Top most delicious "Bun Oc" in Hanoi

❖ Bun Oc Co Hue

Address: 26 Dang Dung, Ba Dinh, Ha Noi

Open: 6:00 am - 2:00 pm

Prices: VND20,000 - 35,000 ~ $0.87 - $1.52

❖ Bun Oc Thuy - Hoe Nhai

Address: 13 Hoe Nhai, Ba Dinh, Ha Noi

Open: 7:00 am - 9:00 pm

Prices: VND30,000 - 40,000 ~ $1.30 - $1.74

❖ Bun Oc Co Ly - Bach Mai

Address: 433 Bach Mai, Hai Ba Trung, Ha Noi

Open: 7:00 am - 3:00 pm

Prices: VND30,000 - 40,000 ~ $1.30 - $1.78

❖ Bun Oc Co Lan

Address: No.26 139, Khuong Thuong, Dong Da, Ha Noi

Open: 7:00 am - 9:00 pm

Prices: VND35,000 - 60,000 ~ $1.52 - $2.6

Street foods

1. Banh Mi Hanoi

"Banh Mi" in the heart of Hanoi old town. It is no longer just a dish, it is also the culinary culture that makes people remember, people like.

This is a very familiar dish and has more spread than any specialty in Vietnam.

Top most delicious "Banh Mi" in Hanoi

❖ Banh Mi Pho Co

Address: 38 Dinh Liet, Hang Dao, Hoan Kiem, Ha Noi

Open: 7:00 am - 12:00 pm

Prices: VND10,000 - 60,000 ~ $0.43 - $2.60

❖ Banh Mi Tram - Hang Bong

Address: 252 Hang Bong, Cua Nam, Hoan Kiem, Ha Noi

Open: 2:00 pm - 11:00 pm

Prices: VND30,000 - 40,000 ~ $1.30 - $1.78

❖ Banh Mi Bao Quyen

Address: No.8 Cha Ca, Hang Bo, Hoan Kiem, Ha Noi

Open: 7:00 am - 10:00 pm

Prices: VND15,000 - 35,000 ~ $0.65 - $1.52

❖ Banh Mi Pho Co - 38 Dinh Liet

Address: 38 Dinh Liet, Hang Dao, Hoan Kiem, Ha Noi

Open: 7:00 am - 3:00 pm

Prices: VND10,000 - 60,000 ~ $0.43 - $2.60

❖ Banh Mi Thit Xien Hoang Duc

Address: 55 Chua Lang, Dong Da, Ha Noi

Open: 11:00 am - 1:00 pm | 4:00 pm - 7:30 pm

Prices: VND20,000 - 50,000 ~ $0.87 - $2.17

2. Banh Cuon (steamed rolled rice pancake)

Banh cuon has long origin and has become a popular dish throughout Vietnam.

It is not difficult to find "Banh Cuon" shops in Hanoi street because "Banh Cuon" are not only loved by Vietnamese but their delicious taste also attracts foreign visitors. Just enjoy that you will never be able to forget.

Top most delicious "Banh Cuon" in Hanoi

❖ Banh Cuon Ba Hanh

Address: 26B Tho Xuong, Hang Trong, Hoan Kiem, Ha Noi

Open: 6:00 am - 03:00 pm | 05:00 pm - 10:00 pm

Prices: VND25,000 - 40,000 ~ $1.08 - $1.74

❖ Banh Cuon Ruoc Tom - Hang Cot

Address: 68 Hang Cot, Hoan Kiem, Ha Noi

Open: 7:00 am - 11:00 am | 04:00 pm - 9:00 pm

Prices: VND30,000 - 65,000 ~ $1.30 - $2.82

❖ Banh Cuon Bao Khanh

Address: 14 Bao Khanh, Hoan Kiem, Ha Noi

Open: 7:00 am - 10:00 pm

Prices: VND15,000 - 35,000 ~ $0.65 - $1.52

❖ Banh Cuon Quang An

Address: 71 Hang Bo, Hoan Kiem, Ha Noi

Open: 05:00 pm - 11:00 pm

Prices: VND30,000 - 55,000 ~ $1.30 - $2.39

3. Banh Gio (pyramidal rice dumpling)

"Banh gio" is a traditional cake of Hanoi people, a famous street food, and usually eaten when it is still hot. Unlike other cakes, "Banh gio" only have a certain shape, which is a pyramid shaped cake and necessarily only wrapped with banana leaves, simple ingredients with rice flour, pork and wood ear.

Top most delicious "Banh gio" in Hanoi

❖ Banh Gio Dong Cac

Address: 33 Dong Cac, Dong Da, Ha Noi

Open: 7:00 am - 7:00 pm

Prices: VND10,000 - 15,000 ~ $0.43- $0.65

❖ Banh Gio Nguyen Cong Tru

Address: 33 Dong Cac, Dong Da, Ha Noi

Open: 7:00 am - 7:00 pm

Prices: VND10,000 - 15,000 ~ $0.43- $0.65

4. Banh Tom (Shrimp crackers)

Shrimp crackers, originally from street vendors, are a popular dish. Later, shrimp cakes were put on sale in elegant and luxurious shops everywhere. Shrimp cake is one of the dishes that make up Hanoi cuisine that any international tourist should try once.

Top most delicious "Banh Tom" in Hanoi

❖ Banh tom Co Am

Address: Ngo Dong Xuan, Hang Chieu, Hoan Kiem , Ha Noi

Open: 2:30 pm - 5:00 pm

Prices: VND10,000 - 50,000 ~ $0.43- $2.17

❖ Banh tom Hang Bo

Address: 55 Hang Bo, Hoan Kiem , Ha Noi

Open: 1:30 pm - 5:00 pm

Prices: VND15,000 - 50,000 ~ $0.65- $2.17

❖ Banh tom Ba Loc

Address: No.1 ngo 26 Nguyen Hong, Dong Da , Ha Noi

Open: 1:30 pm - 10:00 pm

Prices: VND25,000 - 50,000 ~ $1.08- $2.17

❖ Banh tom Nghia Tân

Address: A20 Nghia Tan, Cau Giay , Ha Noi

Open: 1:30 pm - 10:00 pm

Prices: VND25,000 - 50,000 ~ $1.08- $2.17

5. Bánh đúc nóng

Among the famous street foods in Hanoi that are suitable in the winter, hot cakes are mentioned the most.

There is nothing more wonderful than being with friends and relatives enjoying the hot, delicious "bánh đúc" in a small street corner in the cold weather.

Top most delicious "Banh duc nong" in Hanoi

❖ Banh duc nong Le Ngoc Han

Address: No.8 Le Ngoc Han, Ngo Thi Nham, Hai Ba Trung , Ha Noi

Open: 8:30 am - 9:00 pm

Prices: VND25,000 - 30,000 ~ $1.08- $1.30

❖ Banh duc nong Trung Tu

Address: 116C2 Trung Tu, Dong Da , Ha Noi

Open: 4:00 pm - 6:00 pm

Prices: VND10,000 - 15,000 ~ $0.43- $0.65

❖ Banh duc nong Minh Khai

Address: 246 Minh Khai, Hai Ba Trung, Ha Noi

Open: 2:00 pm - 5:00 pm

Prices: VND25,000 - 30,000 ~ $1.08- $1.30

❖ Banh duc nóng Hang Be

Address: 28 Hang Be, Hoan Kiem , Ha Noi

Open: 7:30 am - 9:00 pm

Prices: VND15,000 - 30,000 ~ $0.65- $1.30

Among the many types of drinks in general and coffee in particular in the world, egg coffee still has a very special feature from mixing to enjoy. Anyone who has never tried it will not be able to know the special charm of a type of coffee only available in Vietnam, bearing the unique character of Hanoi.

The harmonious blend, not too sweet, not too bitter, the greasy taste of the egg and the passionate aroma of coffee. Brings extremely interesting experience for those who first taste.

Top most delicious "Egg Coffee" in Hanoi

❖ Dinh Coffee

Address: Floor 2, 13 Dinh Tien Hoang, Hang Bac, Hoan Kiem , Ha Noi

Open: 7:30 am - 10:00 pm

Prices: VND30,000 - 70,000 ~ $1.30- $3.04

❖ Giang Coffee

Address: 39 Nguyen Huu Huan, Hoan Kiem , Ha Noi

Open: 7:30 am - 10:00 pm

Prices: VND15,000 - 35,000 ~ $1.30- $3.04

❖ Lều Coffee

Address: No.1 Ta Hien, Hang Buom, Hoan Kiem , Ha Noi

Open: 9:00 am - 2:00 pm

Prices: VND30,000 - 70,000 ~ $1.30- $3.04

❖ Memory Coffee

Address: 4/37 ngo 82 Chua Lang, Dong Da , Ha Noi

Open: 8:00 am - 10:00 pm

Prices: VND30,000 - 60,000 ~ $1.30- $2.60

❖ Phố Cổ Coffee

Address: 11 Hang Gai, Hoan Kiem , Ha Noi

Open: 8:30 am - 11:00 pm

Prices: VND40,000 - 50,000 ~ $1.73- $2.17

7/ Cốm Hanoi (green rice flakes)

Com is unique to Hanoi, is a Vietnamese cuisine in general and is the most famous specialty of Hanoi in particular. This is a typical product of Vong village (also known as Hau village) which is now Dich Vong Hau ward, Cau Giay district, Hanoi.

Top most delicious "Cốm" in Hanoi

❖ Com Lang Vong Tam Tam

Address: Lang Com Vong, Dich Hau Vong, Cau Giay , Ha Noi

Open: 8:30 am - 10:00 pm

Prices: VND260,000 - 300,000 / kg ~ $11.30- $13.04

❖ Com Me Tri Linh Chi

Address: 66 Me Tri Thuong, nam Tu Liem , Ha Noi

Open: 8:30 am - 10:00 pm

Prices: VND100,000 - 300,000 / kg ~ $4.35- $13.04

❖ Com Moc Me Tri

Address: No.1 Me Tri Thuong, Me Tri , Ha Noi

Open: 8:30 am - 10:00 pm

Prices: VND260,000 - 300,000 / kg ~ $11.30- $13.04

❖ Com Vong Co Man

Address: 86 Tran Thai Tong, Dich Vong Hau, Cau Giay , Ha Noi

Open: 8:30 am - 10:00 pm

Prices: VND260,000 - 300,000 / kg ~ $11.30- $13.04

8/ Trang Tien Ice-cream

Present in Vietnam since 1958, Kem Trang Tien is a unique culture associated with the memories of many Hanoians.

Ice cream shop is open during 4 seasons of the year. In the summer, you can enjoy the cool taste of ice cream; However, in the winter, these creams are not too cold while they can still keep the sweet taste. Many foreign tourists coming to Hanoi must definitely try Trang Tien ice cream once during the trip because of its popularity. The special thing of the ice cream shop is that there is no seat for you to enjoy, so you have to queue in order to buy ice cream, and then have to stand at the store to eat ice cream. This is also a very interesting thing in Hanoi culinary culture.

❖ Address: 35 Trang Tien, Hoa Kiem , Ha Noi

Note: just buy at this address, this is the original store in Hanoi, another stores is the Counterfeiters.

❖ Prices: VND7,000 - 8,000 /piece ~ $0.30- $0.34

A famous dish of Hanoi in particular and the North in general. Bowl of "Cháo Long" hot, full of heart, stomach, liver, blood, heart, ... placed in front of you, listening to the hustle of life on the street and enjoying each spoon of porridge will surely be interesting, right?

Top most delicious "Chao Long" in Hanoi

❖ Chao Long - Thuoc Bac

Address: 88 Thuoc Bac, Hang Bo, Hoan Kiem , Ha Noi

Open: 7:30 am - 12:00 am

Prices: VND20,000 - 60,000 / kg ~ $0.87- $2.6

❖ Chao Long Dao Duy Tu

Address: No.4 Dao Duy Tu, Hoan Kiem , Ha Noi

Open: 3:00 pm - 10:00 pm

Prices: VND30,000 - 60,000 / kg ~ $1.30- $2.6

❖ Chao Long Lo Su

Address: 18 Lo Su, Hoan Kiem , Ha Noi

Open: 11:00 am - 2:00 pm

Prices: VND25,000 - 50,000 / kg ~ $1.08- $2.17

❖ Chao Long Hoa Bang

Address: Ngo 37, Hoa Bang, Cau Giay , Ha Noi

Open: 5:00 pm - 9:00 pm

Prices: VND20,000 - 50,000 / kg ~ $0.87- $2.17

❖ Chao Long Tran Khac Chan

Address: 8265 Tran Khac Chan, Hai Ba Trung, Ha Noi

Open: 7:30 am - 12:00 am

Prices: VND20,000 - 60,000 / kg ~ $0.87- $2.6

10/ Cháo sườn - pork rib porridge

Another excellent street food in the style of Hanoi. This is literally a sidewalk dish, because if you go to a middle-class restaurant, it is very difficult to find "chao suon".

The material for making "chao suon" is quite simple but is processed with a quite rich unforgettable flavor.

If you've visited Hanoi and have plenty of time, you should try experiencing a bowl of "chao suon", I'm sure you will love the taste of it.

Top most delicious "Chao Suon" in Hanoi

❖ Chao Suon Doi Can

Address: 142D Doi Can, Ba Dinh, Ha Noi

Open: 10:00 am - 10:00 pm

Prices: VND25,000 - 50,000 / kg ~ $1.08- $2.17

❖ Chao Suon Ta Quang Buu

Address: 17 T Quang Buu, Hai Ba Trung, Ha Noi

Open: 3:00 pm - 10:00 pm

Prices: VND10,000 - 15,000 / kg ~ $0.43- $0.65

❖ Chao Suon Yen - Ngo Huyen

Address: 43 Ngo Huyen, Hoan Kiem, Ha Noi

Open: 11:00 am - 6:30 pm

Prices: VND15,000 - 30,000 / kg ~ $0.65- $1.30

❖ Chao Suon Huyen Anh

Address: 14 Dong Xuan, Hang Ma, Hoan Kiem, Ha Noi

Open: 6:00 pm - 2:00 am

Prices: VND25,000 - 50,000 / kg ~ $1.08- $2.17

11/ Hoa quả dầm (beam fruits)

It would be flawed not to talk about "beam fruits" in the collection of Hanoi street food. Beam fruits in Hanoi with all kinds of chopped fruits, mixed with condensed milk, yogurt, jelly, fresh cream ... just thinking about it makes me feel cool. Yeahhhh

Take a walk on the streets of Hanoi in the evening and try this wonderful snack.

Top most delicious "beam fruits" in Hanoi

❖ Hoa Qua Dam - Le Thanh Nghi

Address: 36 Le Thanh Nghi, Hai Ba Trung, Ha Noi

Open: 8:00 am - 10:00 pm

Prices: VND20,000 - 30,000 / kg ~ $1.08- $1.30

❖ Hoa Qua Dam Hoa Beo

Address: 17 To Tich, Hoan Kiem, Ha Noi

Open: 8:30 am - 10:00 pm

Prices: VND20,000 - 50,000 / kg ~ $1.08- $2.17

❖ Hoa Qua Dam - Hang Chi

Address: No.5 Hang Chi, Hoan Kiem, Ha Noi

Open: 8:00 am - 10:00 pm

Prices: VND15,000 - 30,000 / kg ~ $0.65- $1.30

❖ Hoa Qua Dam Funny Monkey

Address: 251 Xa Dan, Dong Da, Ha Noi

Open: 8:00 am - 10:00 pm

Prices: VND20,000 - 50,000 / kg ~ $0.86- $2.17

Chapter 6: Attractions around Hanoi

Ba Vi National Park

Ba Vi National Park can be considered an ideal tourist destination because it is not influenced by human hands. Going to Ba Vi Mountain, you need to go through very steep and winding mountain passes, but this trip will bring you the most relaxing moments due to the cool weather and fresh air here.

There are many resorts and resorts here but if you go in groups, camping activities, campfire will bring you the most interesting emotions.

❖ **Location:** Tan Linh Commune, Ba Vi District, Hanoi.

❖ **Ticket price:**

- Adult: VND 40,000 / person, young child: VND 20,000 / person.

- Motorcycle parking ticket: 5,000 VND / unit.

❖ **Note:**

- If camping overnight at the hill, the ticket price per person: 50,000 VND / person

- You should bring barbecue, drinking water and gas before you enter Ba Vi National Park.

- The road to the mountain is quite nice but steep and winding.

Ham Lon mountain - Soc Son

This 426m high pristine mountain is a quite suitable place for trekking addicts, even experienced Fansipan climbers also recommend that climbing Ham Lon Peak is a training step before conquering the roof of Vietnam.

At the top of Ham Lon, there is a spacious ground, lots of green trees and quite flat, suitable for camping and baking.

At the foot of the mountain is the Ham Lon Lake (also known as Suoi Bau Lake), which is quite beautiful among green and pristine pine hills.

❖ **Location:** Located 40km from Hanoi in the direction of North Thang Long - Noi Bai Highway, Ham Lon Mountain in Doc Ton Range, Soc Son.

❖ **Cost:** Services in Ham Lon are quite cheap, if traveling in groups of 4 or more people, the cost is only about 1 million.

❖ **Note:**

- You should prepare ready meals or baked goods when participating in camping on the top of the mountain just because the food service here is not very adequate.

- For those who participate in camping, you should follow the regulations on fire prevention and fighting, putting out the fire after baking food to prevent forest fire.

Three island (Tam Đảo)

Tam Dao is a famous tourist destination and many people know it because the weather is very beautiful, comparable to Sapa and Dalat. Nature has bestowed on Tam Dao a wonderful and dreamlike scenery in the mist of smoke coming from the mountain communal house to every grass and every house.

Over the centuries, but Tam Dao tourist destination still retains the mysterious beauty.

❖ **Location:** Tam Dao tourist area is located in Tam Đảo town, Tam Đảo district, Vĩnh Phúc province, 86km from Hà Nội.

Outstanding destinations: Come here, you can follow the murky stream of clear water to famous spots such as Silver waterfall, Silver stream, Golden stream, Thuong Tay Thien temple ...

❖ **Cuisine:** Tam Dao hill chicken, forest vegetables, Beef is bitten by ants ... are specialties of Tam Dao

❖ **Note:** Food services, hotels in Tam Dao are quite expensive, you should find out before using the service or bringing food at home.

Bat Trang pottery village

As the oldest and most famous pottery village in Vietnam, Bat Trang is a favorite spot for many visitors to experience the traditional culture here.

❖ **Location:** Bat Trang ceramic village is located along the Red River, Gia Lam district, suburban Hanoi. About 10km from Hanoi.

The most interesting point of Bat Trang: you can directly visit the artisans who make extremely rich ceramic products. And especially manually made your favorite products only cost 10.000-20.000 VND.

❖ **Interesting places of interest:** you should visit some of the following points: Bat Trang pottery market, Bat Trang ancient village, taking part in making pottery, Minh Hai resort, Van Van house ....

Huong Pagoda - My Duc

The journey to Huong Pagoda is to the land of Buddhism, Huong Pagoda is a tourist destination around Hanoi that attracts a huge number of tourists during the festive season from January to March of the lunar calendar every year. This is an ideal time for you to enjoy the exciting atmosphere of the Huong Pagoda Festival.

❖ **Note:** This time is also very sensitive because the number of customers is overloaded, the quality of service is poor, pickpockets, security are difficult.

If the purpose is sightseeing, you should avoid the peak time of the festival, so go in late October and early November.

❖ **Location:** Huong Son commune, My Duc district, Hanoi, more than 50km from Hanoi.

❖ **Sights:** There are many attractive destinations such as: Thien Tru, Hinh Bong cave, Oan cave, Huong Tich cave, Thanh Son, Long Van ...

❖ **Food:** There are many restaurants, you should ask the price before eating, the specialties of Huong Pagoda include: bison, mountain goat, horse, porcupine, pangolin, zucchini, ...

Quan Son Lake - My Duc, Hanoi

An attractive tourist destination, Quan Son Lake has a beautiful landscape with limestone mountains by the lake, along with rich vegetation on the water such as lotus, water lily, ...

❖ **Location:** 850ha Ho Quan Son is located in 5 communes, My Duc district, 50km from Hanoi.

❖ **Ideal time:** Mid-May, June of the solar calendar is the best time of the lake because the lotus season is in full bloom.

❖ **Ticket:**

- Entrance fee: VND 15,000 / person

- Around the lake by corrugated boat: 150,000 VND / 4 people.

- Motorcycle parking ticket: 5,000 VND / person

❖ **Interesting point:** In addition to sightseeing, you can also camp in the forest, go boating, fishing, hiking, swimming in the lake ... and enjoy many specialties such as tortoise, fish salad ...

Mineral spring tourist area Kim Boi - Hoa Binh

Kim Boi Resort - Hoa Binh is famous for its natural hot water source, qualified for clean water and temperature for all purposes such as drinking water, bathing water, treatment of bone and joint diseases, blood pressure...

Kim Boi is appropriately designed in the middle of gardens, lakes with fresh air and tranquility.

❖ **Location:** Kim Boi district, Hoa Binh, 70km from Hanoi city.

❖ **Interesting point:** Here you can play tennis, badminton, table tennis and of course, you can not miss the rich bath services: jet bath, whirlpool bath, jacuzzi bath, yin and yang bath, massage combined with mineral bath , therapy, mud bath.

❖ **Cuisine:** The dishes with strong flavors of Northwestern region such as: buffalo meat, chicken with banana cooked, sour bamboo shoot chicken soup, rock mountain goat, aromatic roasted veal, bamboo-tube rice, forest vegetables, ...

❖ **Ticket:**

Price of mineral bathing service: 65,000 VND / time

Hotels: 650,000 - 1,200,000 VND

Trang An - Ninh Binh tourist area

With millions of years old limestone mountains, valleys, caves, lakes, rich mangroves, Trang An tourist area is a must not miss in the list of cheap trips near Hanoi.

With sightseeing cruise activities, you will be immersed in nature to feel the most wonderful gift of heaven and earth to Vietnam.

❖ **Location:** Nho Quan district, Ninh Binh.

❖ **Interesting point:** You will be attracted by the beauty of the majestic cliffs including stalactite sparkling caves, the most attraction of Trang An for tourists is the scenic cruise on the clear blue lake .

❖ **Note:**

To explore Trang An scenic spot, it will take you more than 3 hours by boat. Usually each boat can accommodate from 4-5 people. Ticket price for boat is 150,000 VND/ person. During the high season, a lot of tourists come here to visit, so there is often an overload and crowding at the points of purchase, ticket control and marina. You need to be alert against theft, pickpockets.

Bai Dinh - One of the largest temple in Asia

Bai Dinh Pagoda is a temple complex located on Bai Dinh mountain in Gia Sinh commune, Gia Vien district, about 50km from Hanoi, 12km from Ninh Binh city. Bai Dinh Pagoda has a land area of 539 ha including 27 ha of ancient Bai Dinh pagoda, 80ha of new Bai Dinh pagoda. It is an annual honor to welcome thousands of Buddhists on their pilgrimage.

This is one of the largest temples in Asia and Vietnam with many records being recorded.

From January to March of the lunar calendar when warm spring weather is also the best time to go to Bai Dinh. However, this is also the peak tourist season so visitors here are very crowded, causing overcrowding and crowding. So if you do not like to be busy, noisy, you can also visit Bai Dinh pagoda at other times of the year.

Chapter 7: Shopping in Hanoi

Hanoi city is a perfect choice for those who want to spend all day and night to have fun and shop. This city is a tourist friendly destination with lots of amusement parks, shopping items for tourists. The following list will suggest you the 10 best shopping places in Hanoi you should visit.

Night market in the old town

This is an interesting shopping destination for both locals and tourists at home and abroad.

This market has a large area selling goods starting from Hang Dao Street to Dong Xuan Market. There are nearly 4,000 stalls selling thousands of items such as clothing, shoes, lacquer, souvenirs, jewelry, handicrafts, accessories ... at affordable prices.

The best thing about coming to this night market is that you can experience some traditional street foods such as pho, noodles, fruit beams and traditional cakes .

Old Quarter Night Market is only open from Friday night to Sunday.

❖ **Note when shopping at Old Quarter night market:**

- If possible, you should bargain or consult prices before buying goods here, because the original sellers will sell the price is very high.

- Be careful with your pocket, or your wallet because it's quite crowded here, there have been many cases of pickpockets, jerks during the day.

Hang Ma street

As one of 36 Hanoi Old Quarter, Hang Ma Street is located on the road from Hoan Kiem Lake to Dong Xuan Market. This is one of the bustling streets in the old town, the street sells many kinds of colorful handmade traditional goods, especially the beautifully decorated lanterns.

These items are mostly used to decorate homes. On special occasions such as Christmas, New Year, Chinese New Year or Mid-Autumn Festival, Hang Ma Street is always full of people, both locals and tourists.

This is an ideal destination for you to take photos, to keep good memories when traveling in Hanoi

Hang Duong Street

Hang Duong Street existed before the French colonial period, after the French called rue du Sucre. In 1945, it regained its Vietnamese name of Hang Duong Street, now belonging to Hang Dao Ward, Hoan Kiem District, Hanoi.

As one of the busiest streets of the 36 streets in Hanoi, Hang Duong Street is the place to sell a variety of snacks and sweets to everyone. Especially, O Mai - the most famous specialty snacks in Hanoi, is sold very much in Hang Duong.

Van Phuc silk village

Van Phuc silk village is 10 km from the center of Hanoi with pictures of old houses and stone roads that were popular in Vietnam for decades.

In addition to the beautiful scenery, Van Phuc village is also famous for international silk production and trade. Silk was created by skillful and intelligent weavers in Van Phuc village.

Every year, Van Phuc Village attracts thousands of domestic and foreign tourists coming here to buy the best quality silk products.

❖ **Note when buying silk in Van Phuc:**

- There are many Chinese silk products in Van Phuc village and you should come and learn the big and reputable shops to get the best genuine products.

- Genuine silk is very soft and thin. Whenever you try, you can totally feel the smooth and comfortable silk.

- Do not be surprised with the genuine silk prices. As the saying "you get what you pay for?", The higher you pay, the better the silk. However, remember to bargain for a better price.

Hang Be Market

Hang Be Market near Hoan Kiem Lake is one of the famous shopping places in Hanoi. Every day, a large number of people come to Hang Be market to search for necessary items and shopping.

Besides the delicious food, fashion clothes and local souvenirs, Hang Be Market is also a cultural exchange where you can see groups of foreigners walking around the market. These tourists and foreigners see Hang Be market as a real destination to discover Vietnamese lifestyle.

❖ **Address:** No.4 Nguyen Thien Thuat, Hang Bac, Hoan Kiem, Ha Noi

AEON Shopping Center

Located next to Vinh Tuy Bridge area of Long Bien district, AEON shopping mall has 2 fronts facing two main roads, namely Co Linh and Dam Quang Trung.

This shopping center is a great place for shoppers. AEON has hundreds of stalls selling items from high-end to affordable

In addition to selling shopping items, AEON also has a lot of entertainment services such as dining, cinemas, game areas ...

❖ **Address:** 27 Hong Tien, Long Bien, Ha Noi

❖ **Open:** 10:00 am - 10:00 pm

Vincom Mega Mall Royal City

This is the largest underground shopping center in Hanoi. This is a paradise for shopaholics. The mall is so wide you will need a map to keep yourself from getting lost.

Make sure you are ready for a shopping day, Vincom will have everything you need. The products here range from personal items to household appliances, high fashion to modern technology products. Take a few hours to enjoy the wonderful shopping atmosphere in Vincom.

❖ **Address:** 72A Nguyen Trai, Thuong Dinh, Thanh Xuan, Ha Noi

❖ **Open:** 9:30 am - 10:00 pm

La Spa Trendy Spa & Massage

Address: 10 Nguyen Quang Bich, Cua Dong, Hoan Kiem, Hanoi.

Open: 9:00am - 9:00pm

Alisa Bella Spa Hanoi

Address: 4B Ma May , Hang Buom, Hoan Kiem, Hanoi.

Open: 9:00am - 9:00pm

Lotus Spa Hanoi

Address: 36 Ma May , Hang Buom, Hoan Kiem, Hanoi.

Open: 9:00am - 10:00pm

MF Boutique Spa & Wellness Hanoi

Address: 191 Hang Bong, Hoan Kiem, Hanoi.

Open: 9:00am - 10:00pm

Mido Spa

Address: 11A Hang Be, Hoan Kiem, Hanoi.

Open: 9:00am - 10:00pm

Midori Spa - Gia Ngu

Address: 28 Gia Ngu, Hoan Kiem, Hanoi.

Open: 9:00am - 10:00pm

Serene Spa

Address: 68 Ma May, Hoan Kiem, Hanoi.

Open: 9:00am - 10:00pm

Chapter 9: Travel Tips

1/ Buy travel insurance

The most important piece of safety advice I can offer is to purchase good travel insurance. Travel insurance will protect you against illness, injury, theft, and cancellations. It's comprehensive protection in case anything goes wrong. I never go on a trip without it.

2/ Choose clothes when traveling Hanoi

If you come in the summer, you should choose compact clothes, sweat quickly, wear a cap, wide brim because the weather is very hot, plus the hot asphalt and dust from traffic will make you very exhausted. On the contrary, if it is winter, you must prepare a cold coat because sometimes the temperature drops below 10 degrees.

Another note is that Hanoi has many temples, so if you want to wear skirts or shorts, you should wear a large scarf to wrap around your feet when coming here. But it is still best to wear a discreet, polite outfit.

3/ Do not forget the necessary items

Not only in Hanoi, but wherever you are, taking an inventory of the necessary items is always an obligatory action of each trip. Identity documents such as your identity card, driver's license, notebooks for taking notes should be put in a briefcase first. You should spend a small space to store medicines, especially digestive drugs, because when eating the strange foods, you will be prone to abdominal pain. Also bring cotton, personal bandages, they will never be redundant.

4/ Shopping

Souvenirs are considered "indispensable" after each trip, you can find these easily in Hanoi. Marketplaces are often sold at high prices for tourists, so you maybe bargain when choosing to buy something. You can consult prices before going shopping, through online search or asking the local people you know.

Note: At markets, if you just want to see the goods, don't come in the morning. Most Vietnamese believe that the first guest will affect that day's trade. If you shop early in the morning, please avoid bargaining. If possible, buy a small item and have fun chatting with the owner. This can help you avoid trouble from the impolite and difficult salesman who will have unpleasant words that make you lose interest and discomfort (In my opinion, better not to buy or see the product in the early morning).

5/ Preventing fraud and theft

Be on alert for scams. Because many people think, as a tourist, you have a lot of money. So they are really just going to try to get you to pay extra money.

Always trust your instincts. If a taxi driver seems shady, request stop and get out. If your hotel is bad than you thought, get out of there. Make copies of your personal documents, including your passport and ID to prevent theft.

Especially, should not bring too much cash with you, theft in Hanoi is quite common. So it's best to bring an ATM card, because Hanoi has many card stations of many different banks, both compact and secure to avoid theft.

6/ Always check price before using any services

Asking prices is obviously something you must do first when you step into the restaurant or use any service, because this is an effective way to "protect" your wallet.

7/ Credit card

Today, hackers don't just sit behind a computer screen. Some hackers steal bank card data right in front of visitors. In fact, there was the case that the shopkeepers, restaurant servants or hotel receptionists intended to use the phone to capture the numbers on your credit card, then rob money in that.

Therefore, you should keep an eye on cards when giving them to strangers, do not give your cards to those who hold the phones in their hands.

8/ When taking a taxi

During the journey of the trip, you need a map (or smart phone with google map), which is very helpful in traveling or estimating taxi fees.

You need to choose reputable taxi companies. Popular taxi price is about VND 12,000 for opening, and about VND 16,000 per next kilometre. When you get on the car, you should keep eyes on the driver, maybe most of the drivers are honest people but some are cheating drivers, they will charge twice, triple. They will take you roundabouts to increase fees, or take you to the restaurants, hotels that they know and charge for rooms, meals much higher than the normal price.

- Sometimes they may want to confuse you and claim you only gave VND10,000 although you have paid VND100,000 .

- Hold your wallet away from any driver to make it impossible to grab your money with his hand to "help you". Do not let a driver count your money for you. Speak out the amount you just paid and get their confirmation.

Worst case, you should take a photo of their Taxi ID and ask someone to call their company later.

- If you can use apps on phone like Grab, Be, Fastgo, it is great, you will never have to fear being cheated on price.

9/ Public water

No same many other countries, we cannot drink water directly from fountains in Vietnam, the safest way is to buy a bottle of mineral water at stores or supermarkets.

10/ Absolutely not give money to beggars

NO, I repeat NOT give money to beggars (even children, the elderly or people with disabilities), no matter how poor they seem. This is not for any inhumane or unjustified reason, just because most of these beggars are part of the "beggar system", often be led by some unethical people (believe it or not, there are still monsters out there who use children to make money for them). If you think you give money directly to beggars for helping them? You are wrong, you are nurturing this system.

The best way to handle this situation is to pretend that they are invisible. If you say "no" or answer, they will continue to bother you until you agree to give them money. If you ignore them, they will give up and disappear.

11/ Train

- Buy tickets early for cheaper prices and seat as expected.

- If you go a long way, should be choose sleeper train. Train Seat is for short distances.

- When the ship arrives at the station, there will be a lot of street vendors going on board to sell. Do not buy their goods, because they are not good and you can be cheated.

-Each wagon has only one toilet, so many people need to use it. Avoid "rush hour" because it can take a lot of time, for example 6 -7 a.m when people wake up and do personal hygiene.

- On the train will have mobile "canteen" pushed by two attendants, they sell food and drinks. Of course the price will be more expensive than normal, sometimes not delicious. So I recommend bringing some backup food like instant noodles, snacks. Hot water is available on train. It is also interesting to eat and watch outside.

- When boarding a train, store your luggage neatly. Before getting off the train, you must check carefully.

12/ Money Tips

Tipping is almost inevitable in Vietnam, you will find that employees will be more happy and enthusiastic if you give them tip.

- Hotel staff: VND20,000 - 50,000 ~$1.00 - 2.00

- Restaurant staff: maybe or not, VND20,000 - 50,000 ~$1.00 - 2.00

- Drivers: VND10,000 - 30,000

- Massage healthy/ foot massage (not service a-z massage): VND100,000 - 200,000 ~ $4.00 - 8.00.

13/ Lunar New Year - TET

This is the traditional Tet holiday in Vietnam. At this time, many hotels, dining outlets and services will be closed for about 5-7 days. Some places are still open, but the price may be higher than usual, you should ask the price before using.

14/ Rush hour

Referring to traffic jams, Hanoi people see it as a horrifying thing. Try to drive to the street at the hour of about 5 pm to 6 pm or from 11 a.m -12 a.m, you will witness people and cars crowded like a maze. Therefore, at peak hours, choose a walk or stop to rest or choose other time to explore this magnificent city.

15/ Crossing the road

Crossing the road in Vietnam, is considered a risky but exciting challenge. There are two cases when you cross the street:

❖ 1: You cross the road at an intersection with traffic lights and a priority line for people crossing the road:

This is a simple case, you just have to wait for the red light, the car stops and walks over. However, there are many case that motorcycles still turn right when the lights are red (although this is illegal), so you still have to pay attention to avoid them.

❖ 2: You cross the road where there is no traffic light and priority line for people crossing the road:

This case, you just walk down the road and slowly cross the street. You should raise one hand as a signal, keeping your eyes in the direction of the vehicles approaching you, and pay attention to the speed of them. If vehicles slow down, they intend to give way to you, they will stop or run behind you. If vehicles do not change or speed up, you should stop.

Do not run. Do not drop back suddenly. You can ask a local person to take you across the road several times until you get used to it.

❖ Note: In Vietnam, not many people pay attention priority lines. So you will not prioritized when crossing the road.

16/ Familiarize yourself with the unpleasant personality of Hanoi people

Perhaps due to cultural differences, you will not be satisfied with the service attitude of Hanoi people. I myself was really shocked with the service attitude of some shops in Hanoi when I first came here. However, after a period of understanding and explanation of the local people, I learned that this is part of the cultural influence from the feudal period of a small part of Hanoi people, not the whole. The service attitude may not be good, but the quality of the food is still very good.

If you are coming to Hanoi for the first time, it is inevitable that what I have mentioned above, the advice is to skip, as if no problem happened and enjoy your trip. After all, you don't want to be annoyed by what you already knew it would happen, right? It is simply a cultural difference.

Conclusion

Thanks again for reading my book. I hope the informations in this book will be helpful and help you have a pleasant trip.

Now, enjoy your trip.

-- Jason Nguyen –

CHECK OUT OTHER BOOKS

Go here to check out other related books that might interest you:

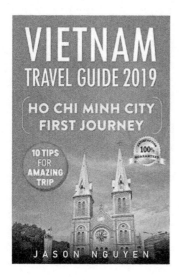
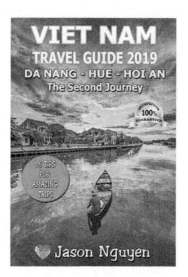

https://www.amazon.com/dp/1099986982

https://www.amazon.com/dp/1081499419

Printed in Great Britain
by Amazon

84978511R10078